D1576960

THE
FULHAM
FC
MISCELLANY

Alex White

The History Press

First published in 2012 by

The History Press
The Mill, Brimscombe Port
Stroud, Gloucestershire, GL5 2QG
www.thehistorypress.co.uk

British Library Cataloguing in Publication Data.
A catalogue record for this book is available from the British Library.

ISBN 978 0 7524 6526 5

Typesetting and origination by The History Press
Printed in Great Britain

INTRODUCTION

This year I celebrate 50 years of watching Fulham. It has had it ups and downs but the last ten years have made up for the years of mediocrity that came before. Being only ten and coming from a family that did not have much money and who were more interested in the arts, I could not afford to watch the club regularly until 1965. I recently worked out that by May 2012 I had seen Fulham's first team play 1,183 times at Craven Cottage and on top of this are a number of away matches plus reserve and junior matches that I have seen at the Cottage and elsewhere. When I first started watching the Cottagers they were a First Division side with some wonderful players such as the great Johnny Haynes plus England's World Cup winning full-back George Cohen, John Dempsey, Tony Macedo, Jim Langley, Alan Mullery, Eddie Lowe, Bobby Robson, Tosh Chamberlain and my favourite Scottish International Graham Leggat. It took me some time to recover after the Fulham manager Vic Buckingham sold him to Birmingham City in January 1967 after scoring five goals in his last two games for the club.

Fulham have always been a quirky club with a great history. We may not have won much over the years but there have been many golden moments to remember. However, there have also been some awful memories of incompetent teams and poor management. My own personal rock-bottom moment came at Scarborough on 1 April 1995 when Fulham managed to lose 3–1 to a team that no longer exists. Of the 52 travelling supporters, I knew 38 of them. They were mostly diehards who rarely missed a match home and away.

My greatest moment as a Fulham fan was the amazing comeback against Juventus in the Europa Cup in 2010. After losing 3–1 in Turin and then conceding an early goal in the return leg, Fulham made an amazing comeback to win 4–1, which included a wonder goal from hero USA international Clint Dempsey. Other great moments have been getting to a Wembley FA Cup final for the one and only time in 1975 – I was at Maine Road when John Mitchell scored with virtually the last kick of the match for the only goal of the semi-final replay against Birmingham City. Also Fulham's rise from the fourth tier to the Premier League in only five seasons had many memorable moments.

From its early days as a church football team, through the golden period of the late 1950s and early '60s to the 33 year wait for the return of top-flight football in 2001, the Lilliewhites have more than held their own ever since and thanks to the generosity of chairman Mohamed Al Fayed, the club has also reached the final of a major European competition.

I hope you enjoy the book.

Alex White, July 2012

FIRST MATCH

The first known match involving a Fulham side is a 4–2 home defeat against Stanley at Eel Brook Common on 6 October 1883. It now seems likely that although former Fulham footballer and secretary Henry Shrimpton's book on the formation and early years of the club states that they were formed in 1879, St Andrew's did not start playing competitive football until 1883 when a cricket club was also formed. There are strong arguments for Fulham's formation date being 1883 rather than 1879. However, there is no definitive proof for either argument.

WEST LONDON CUP

Fulham won 21 of the 22 games that they played during 1886/87 and scored 87 goals, conceding just 13. That season they beat Oaklands 2–0 to reach the first ever West London Cup final where they played St Matthew's in February 1887. The match was played at Ranelagh House with a large crowd present. There was controversy before the match as St Andrew's selected a player called Gamble on the right wing who usually played for St Mark's College (Chelsea). This was his one and only game for the club and he helped St Andrew's to a 2–1 victory. St Matthew's took the lead when Stiles opened the scoring after about 20 minutes but then opposition player Mason broke his collarbone after a clash with Aram and had to leave the pitch. Fulham took advantage of the extra man and scored twice in the last

10 minutes through Jack Howland to win the match. Gamble set up the winner with a fine run down the left and an excellent centre for Howland to head home.

The following season, St Andrew's lost the West London Cup final to Oaklands after a replay. The first game ended in a 1–1 draw with a goal scored by 'Tubby' Carter before a crowd of 600 at the North Kensington Ground. They were outplayed in the replay, losing 4–0 at the same venue, three weeks later. The team was: May; Hobson, Walters; Pearce, Aram, King; Martin, Carter, Andrews, Draper and Maxfield with Newport and Balster replacing Draper and Andrews in the replay. To reach the final they beat Caxtonians 11–0 with goals from Howland (4), Martin (4), Andrews (2) and Aram, and Willesden Junction Institute 7–0 in the semi-finals. Over the next four seasons, Fulham St Andrew's lost on each occasion to great local rivals Stanley FC before they could reach the final.

WEST LONDON OBSERVER CUP

The West London Observer Cup was sponsored by the local newspaper of that name. In its initial season of 1890/91, Fulham reached the final to play Stanley FC. In the first round they defeated West London Tailors 6–3 then beat Kensal 6–1 at Brondesbury in the semi-final with goals from Abon Sermon (3), Tim Draper and Billy Mugford (2). Both finals against Stanley were played at the Half Moon ground in Lower Richmond Road, Putney. The first final, played on 4 April 1891, ended in a 0–0 draw but Fulham won the replay

5–3 a week later thanks to a hat-trick from Billy Mugford and a brace from Tim Draper. The Fulham team for both games was: Jack May; Jack King, Tom Shrimpton; A. Lovell, Joe Chell, George Pearce; Billy Mugford, Tim Draper, Frank Withington, Abon Sermon, Fred Carter.

The following season Fulham lost 2–1 to Stanley in the final at the Kensal Rise Athletic Grounds after beating St John's (Hammersmith) 6–0 and Salisbury (Fulham) 3–1 on the way. Their team in the final was: Jack May; Tom Shrimpton, Jack King; Joe Chell, George Pearce, Arthur Newport; Will Sermon, J. Morrison, F. Smith, Fred Carter, Abon Sermon.

Fulham beat St Clement 3–1 and Salisbury (Fulham) 3–0 before being defeated by Queens Park Rangers 3–2 on 22 April 1893 in the final at the National Athletic Ground at Kensal Rise. The Fulham line up this time was: J. May; T. Shrimpton, T. Curry; T. Cardross, A. Newport, J. King; G. Pearce, A. Fearon, F. Withington, W. King and A. Sermon.

WEST LONDON LEAGUE

Fulham won the newly formed West London League in 1892/93, winning 16 of their 18 matches. They beat QPR 1–0 at their home ground at the Half Moon, Putney, and drew 2–2 in the return match. Their biggest win of the season came at Hounslow, who were beaten 6–1. Their side included the King brothers – Jake and Will, Tom & Jack Shrimpton, secretary Arthur Newport, the excellent goalkeeper Jack May, the Revd Gilbert Montague Hall, Tubby Carter and Horace Wilkins.

EARLY FRIENDLIES

Fulham entered a cup for the first time in 1885, but lost to Hendon 9–0 in the London FA Cup. They entered a league for the first time in 1892 when they joined the West London League. Their main rivals before the turn of the twentieth century were Stanley FC who Fulham met many times in cup and friendly matches. Some of their other opposition in the early days had unusual names such as Reindeer, Venetians, Orion Gymnasium, Aldenham Institute and the Royal School of Mines. Millwall Rovers were the first future Football League club to play Fulham in September 1888. They later became known as Millwall Athletic and then plain Millwall, as they are known today. The match with Millwall was abandoned at half time after all three balls that were available had burst, with Fulham leading 2–1.

The Lilliewhites went on their first tour over Easter 1892 when they visited the West Country for the weekend. They met Weymouth, Yeovil and a South Devon XI at the County Ground in Dorchester. On 15 April 1892 they drew 0–0 with Weymouth and the team was J. May; T.W. Shrimpton, W. Ridout; A. Newport, A.T. Norman, J. McKenzie; A. Mason, H.C. Brewer (Highgate Harriers), A. Morris, F. Carter, J. McDonald. Only Jack May, Tom Shrimpton, Arthur Newport, Tom Norman and Fred 'Tubby' Carter were actual Fulham players – the rest were ringers as many of the Fulham regulars either could not get time off work or could not afford the trip. The following day a South Dorset XI beat Fulham 2–1 with R. Grant of Weymouth replacing the injured Brewer. On Easter Monday, and after a rest day, Fulham played Yeovil and won 3–1 thanks to goals from Mason and Carter (2).

GROUNDS

Before Fulham started playing at Craven Cottage in October 1896 they played at a number of other ground, most of which were not enclosed. Fulham were not able to take a proper gate until they moved to the Half Moon Ground on Lower Richmond Road, Putney, in September 1891. This ground was between the Half Moon pub on Lower Richmond Road and the River Thames. The club shared this ground with Wasps Rugby Union Club until 1895 when it was redeveloped into the houses which stand there today.

The first pitch that St Andrew's played on was little more than a muddy field close to where the club was formed at St Andrew's Church, Star Road, West Kensington. They started to play organised friendly matches in 1883 on Eel Brook Common which was part of a local park and the following year they moved to a ground at Lillie Road, close to the Queens Club. The exact location of this pitch is unknown but it was a different ground than that which had been used for an early FA Cup final that was close to this location. Shortly afterwards the club moved to Lower Putney Common – an open ground on common land.

The football club changed their name to Fulham St Andrew's to distinguish themselves from the many other clubs called St Andrew's in London area. They played at Ranelagh House for two seasons from 1886 to 1888 until the site was used for housing. This ground was situated close to the River Thames by the Hurlingham Club and they used the Eight Bells public house in Fulham High Street for changing rooms. The first known match at Ranelagh House was reported in the *West London Advertiser* for a game with local rival Stanley FC on 23 October 1886. Fulham St Andrew's won the game 5–0 and the team was given as: Jack May; Jack King, Will Hobson; Wilf Hobson, Bert Aram, Tom Norman; Albert Keefe; Fred Carter, Jack Howland, William Andrews and Billy Balster.

The Ranelagh Club, along with Fulham St Andrew's, had to relocate in summer 1888 to Barn Elms, Castelnau (an area that was on the opposite side of the river to the present Craven Cottage ground), owing to the redevelopment of their grounds. The club changed their name to just plain Fulham in December 1888 but attendances dropped off due to the difficulties of getting across the river to the new ground, so Fulham moved to Roskell's Field in 1890 which was close to the Parsons Green tube station. The teams used the Rose & Crown public house as changing rooms but the big drawback at this venue was that the pitch had a tree on it! They returned temporarily to Eel Brook Common in January 1891 as Roskell's Field seemed to be continually waterlogged and many games had to be postponed, then on to the Half Moon in the summer. This was a properly enclosed ground and local cup finals were often played here. When they lost the Half Moon ground in 1895, Fulham played for a season at great local rivals Stanley's home ground at Halford Road, Walham Green, before finding a new home at Craven Cottage.

LONDON LEAGUE

Fulham joined the London League Division Two in 1896 but finished only eighth out of nine teams in their first season. The first match was a 6–1 defeat at Brentford and the first match at the Cottage was an 8–0 defeat against their great local rivals Stanley FC. Goalkeeper Jack May was blamed for this heavy defeat and walked out of the club for a while. Fulham did better in their second season when they finished as runners-up, a point behind champions Barnet. E.H. Freeman scored 23 goals in only 16 appearances and Billy Ives scored 11 goals as Harrow Athletic were beaten 13–0, Forest Swifts 9–0 and Orient 6–0. Fulham appeared in the first division of the London League from 1900 to 1904 as they had so few Southern League fixtures. The reserves played in the London League Division Two from 1904 to 1914 and won the title in 1904/05 and 1913/14.

LONDON SENIOR CUP

Fulham entered the London Senior Cup from 1891 to 1899 but never won the competition for the leading amateur sides in London. Their best season was when they reached the fifth round in 1897/98 before losing to Barking Woodville 1–0 at the Cottage after a 0–0 away draw. They had beaten Westminster 4–1, Wandsworth 1–0, Metropolitan Railway 2–0 and QPR 4–3 to reach the fifth round.

Fighting broke out between the fans of the two clubs when Fulham beat Brentford 1–0 in the London Senior Cup on

9 November 1895. Unfortunately, the dressing rooms were some way from the pitch and a number of Fulham players were assaulted trying to get to safety. Alec Frame had scored the winning goal for Fulham in a tempestuous match. Unfortunately Fulham went on to lose 4–3 to Ealing in the next round after being 3–1 up at the interval.

MIDDLESEX SENIOR CUP

Fulham entered the Middlesex Senior Cup from 1891 to 1897 but rarely did well in the competition. Their best season was 1896/97 when they reached the fourth round. They beat Minerva 4–0 in the first round which was actually also the first ever game at Craven Cottage in October 1896. Jimmy Lindsay, Abon Sermon (2) and Eddie Witheridge scored the goals. Fulham won 3–0 at Enfield in the next round with Sammy Aylott scoring twice and Freddie Hollands also on target. However, they then lost 3–1 to London Welsh in the third round ('Robbie' Robertson scoring) but were later awarded the tie for reasons unknown. Fulham lost to Ealing 3–1 at the Cottage in the fourth round before a crowd of 3,000, L.J. Moon scoring Fulham's only goal. This is believed to be Leonard James Moon who played cricket for Cambridge University and Middlesex. Moon was later ordered to play for the Third Grenadiers rather than Fulham, much to his annoyance, after scoring 5 goals in the first two games of 1897/98. He attended Westminster School and later Pembroke College, Cambridge, from 1897 to 1900 and gained a Blue at football. He also played for the amateurs against the professionals in 1905 and appeared for the Corinthians. Leonard played 63 matches for Middlesex CCC between 1899 and 1903 and toured North America with the MCC in 1905. He was killed on active service in Karasouli, Salonika, Greece, on 23 November 1916.

GOING PROFESSIONAL

Fulham FC turned professional on 12 December 1898 but this decision was not universally accepted at the club and a number of players and committee men walked out, including the Shrimptons who had played a very important role in the development of the club. The Fulham flyer William Robertson (whose family owned Robertson's Jams) and top scorer E.H. Freeman (who was connected to Falstaff Cigars) also walked out. Fulham had to sign new players quickly but none of the signings made in that first month of professionalism stayed very long with the club.

The first signings were John Love from Trowbridge Town who had previously played for Rochdale and New Brighton Tower, and Albert Lewis from Grays United who had appeared just once for the Reds and previously played for Gravesend United and Woolwich Arsenal reserves. However, the third signing stayed a little longer, left-back James McKie from Cowes, who had previously played for Freemantle, Southampton and Chatham.

If the decision to turn professional had not been taken Fulham would probably no longer exist as their great local rivals of the time, Stanley FC, folded shortly afterwards.

THE SHRIMPTONS

The Shrimpton brothers played an important role in the early history of Fulham FC. Not only did they play for the club but they also helped run it in the 1890s. Their involvement with Fulham ended when they left in protest at the decision to turn professional in December 1898. Henry Shrimpton wrote *The Foundation History of Fulham FC* in 1950 and died six years later at the age of 81. A mechanical engineer by trade, he was known as 'Mo' and played occasionally under the name of S.D. Henry due to work commitments. He appeared for the club from 1895 to 1898 and was also honorary secretary for a while.

Older brother Tom Shrimpton made his debut as far back as September 1887 against Wimbledon Rangers in a 3–2 defeat at Fulham's ground at Ranelagh House. He played in three West London Observer Cup finals from 1891 to 1893, gaining one winners' and two losers' medals and also represented West London as a left-back.

Another brother called Jack appeared for Fulham from 1891 to 1893 as an outside left. When Jack was the club secretary in 1896 he was once forced to play in his normal clothes when three players did not turn up for a game with Spurs reserves!

Jim Shrimpton turned out for Fulham occasionally but was usually captain of the Swan Brewery Club. Tom and Henry appeared for Fulham in their first match at Craven Cottage in October 1896. In more recent years a grandson, David Shrimpton, was a director of Fulham.

FULHAM'S BOER WAR SOLDIERS

Fulham's top scorer in 1899/1900 was David Lloyd who had joined the club from Thames Ironworks in July 1899. He then scored 27 goals in all games in 1900/01. As well as being a semi-professional footballer, Lloyd was also a soldier with the Third Grenadiers and when the Boer War began he left the country to fight in South Africa along with team-mates George Sherran and Fred Hopkinson. He appeared in most positions for the Reds and he even played in goal against Maidenhead in April 1901. He was sent off for retaliation during an FA Cup tie against Watford in November 1902 after punching an opponent called Murray, being suspended for 28 days. Lloyd left the Cottage for Willesden Town in August 1904.

BIGGEST DEFEATS

Embarrassingly, Fulham's record defeat came against Millwall's reserve side in a London League fixture on Christmas Day 1900, Fulham losing 11–0. Some of the players must have celebrated the festivities too well the night before as their performance was described as 'a disgrace and shocking' by club officials.

SOUTHERN LEAGUE ABANDONMENTS

Before joining the Football League, there were a number of games that were abandoned or had to be replayed during the Whites' Southern League days. The first of these took place on 19 January 1901 when Chesham United were the visitors to the Cottage. Fulham won 4–1 with goals from Fred Holmes (2), Fred Molyneux and Tommy Meade but this match had to be replayed after Chesham's protests about the referee, who had replaced the official one, were upheld by the league authorities. The original referee had failed to arrive and the replacement was a Fulham official.

On 30 March 1901 the Cottagers were losing 3–0 at Loakes Park against Wycombe Wanderers when the match was abandoned after 45 minutes. Strangely, Fulham were forced to play two Southern League matches on this day owing to a fixture congestion and their side was made up from reserve team players. No reason was given for the abandonment.

The Lilliewhites won 4–1 against Grays United on 27 December 1902 at the Cottage and star striker Tommy Meade had scored all 4 goals. However, the match was ordered to be replayed after Fulham played an unregistered player called Easter at outside left.

Fulham were drawing 1–1 at home against Kettering on 23 January 1903, with a goal from Harry Fletcher, when the match was abandoned after 45 minutes owing to fog. The low attendance of 2,000 had seen very little of the match anyway.

Finally, on 26 November 1904, the match was abandoned against Brentford because of bad weather when Fulham were leading through a goal from Alex Fraser.

AMATEUR INTERNATIONALS

Fulham had their fair share of amateur internationals before this status was abandoned in 1974. Twenty-one Fulham-connected players gained amateur international caps in all, but only four have done so while on the club's books – Bobby Brown, Arthur Berry, Frank Monk and Fred Wheatcroft.

R.H. Brown joined Fulham from Barnet in 1960 and remained an amateur until he left the club the following year. Bobby won 14 caps and played for Great Britain in the 1960 Olympic Games. Future barrister Arthur Berry won his 32 caps while playing with Oxford University, Everton, Fulham, Liverpool and Oxford City from 1907 to 1913. Frank Monk never appeared in the first team after joining Fulham from Southampton in 1911 but played twice for England while at the Cottage. Fred Wheatcroft played once for England before signing as a professional with Derby County in February 1907.

COLOURS

Fulham's usual colours of white shirts and black shorts were first used in 1903 when the club became a limited company. The reasons for using these colours are unknown but the owners had clearly decided to change the image of the club. They had played in Arsenal's colours of red shirts with white sleeves and white shorts from 1896 to 1903, but prior to this they did not have set colours – at one time they'd played in thin black and white striped shirts and earlier had appeared in light blue and dark blue squares.

CORINTHIANS

The Corinthians were the most famous amateur side before the Second World War and consisted of former Oxford and Cambridge University students, many of whom represented their universities at football. They were often good enough to beat league sides in friendly matches and the FA Cup, and Fulham met them on two occasions. Their first encounter came in December 1903 when the Whites were defeated at the Queens Club at nearby Barons Court, before a crowd of 2,000. The Corinthians won 6–2 with Albert Soar and Alf Harwood scoring for Fulham.

The other meeting came in December 1919 when Fulham won 3–2 at the Cottage with goals from Donald Cock, a rare goal from full-back Alec Chaplin and another from guest amateur outside left Gandar-Dower before 7,000 spectators.

REVAMPED COTTAGE

During the summer of 1905 Craven Cottage was completely transformed and rebuilt. The local council condemned the old orange box stand as being unsafe and unsuitable for football – the supports and rafters always obstructed the view of the game at a vital moment. This was replaced by the imposing steel structure that you see today. It measured 382ft in length and 40ft from front to back, and its capacity, including a concrete terraced enclosure, was 5,000, all under cover. Around the rest of the ground, concrete terracing replaced earth mounds, which had proved so dangerous for a cup tie with Reading earlier that year. The new Craven Cottage with its accommodation for players and officials, as well as the red brick frontage and turnstiles on the Stevenage Road end, were built in a little over four months – a remarkable achievement. The red brick frontage was recently refurbished with the help of finances from the Fulham 2000 project. The Cottage was also extensively rebuilt and refurbished.

FULHAM'S EMINENT PSYCHIATRIST

Leslie Skene was Fulham's first goalkeeper after they joined the Football League in 1907. He went on to make 94 appearances for the club before departing for Glentoran in 1910. Skene was educated at George Watson's College, Edinburgh, and at Edinburgh University, where he graduated with a MB and ChB in 1911. After graduation he held the appointment of assistant physician at the Lanark District Asylum, and in 1913 he was among the first to obtain the Diploma in Psychiatry from Edinburgh University. During the First World War he served as a captain in the RAMC, and was twice wounded during the Gallipoli campaign. Skene was awarded the Military Cross for gallantry and distinguished service in the field in the 1918 New Year Honours.

In the years immediately after the war, Skene was a successful medical superintendent at the Perth Criminal Mental Hospital and senior assistant physician at Tooting Bec Mental Hospital. From 1922 to 1947, he was medical superintendent of the Isle of Man Mental Hospital. A member of the British Medical Association for forty years, he was president of the Isle of Man Branch in 1935/6.

FIRST FRIENDLY FOREIGN OPPOSITION

The first foreign opposition to play at Craven Cottage were the touring Sparta Rotterdam side on Good Friday 1903. The Dutch quickly established a 2-goal lead by the interval but Fulham made a comeback to win 3–2 with goals from full-back 'Cabbo' Dwight (penalty), David Lloyd and Tommy Meade.

LIMITED LIABILITY

Fulham became a limited company with a share of capital of £7,500 in May 1903. The club had been unable to move up to the first division of the Southern League as they had lost to Brentford 7–2 in a Test match after finishing the season as Second Division Champions. The Southern League committee informed them that if they could raise a first-class team by 30 May 1903 then promotion would be guaranteed. To enable the club to buy the players, Fulham had to raise capital, thus they became a limited company. The most famous player to be signed was goalkeeper Jack Fryer who had played in the 1903 FA Cup final for Derby County, in which he had let in a record 6 goals after being injured early in the game. New players came mainly from Football League clubs including established professionals such as Harry Fletcher and Peter Gray from Grimsby Town, Jock Hamilton from Bristol City, Fergus Hunt from Woolwich Arsenal and Billy Orr from Manchester City.

FULHAM'S FIRST INTERNATIONAL

Joe Connor became Fulham's first ever international when he appeared for Ireland against England on 12 March 1904. Connor was, at that time, playing for Fulham's reserves so it was a surprise choice. He had previously won two other caps for his country while playing for Brentford. Ireland lost to England 3–1 but Connor had scored on his international debut against Scotland the year before in a 2–0 victory at Hampden Park. Connor served in the Gordon Highlanders before becoming a professional footballer with West Bromwich Albion. He also played for Walsall, Bristol City and Woolwich Arsenal before joining Fulham from New Brompton (now Gillingham) in October 1903 in an exchange deal that saw Alex Davidson moving in the opposite direction.

BIGGEST WIN

Fulham's biggest ever win came in January 1897 when they beat Harrow Athletic 13–0 in a London League Division Two fixture with Freeman hitting 5 and Billy Ives scoring a hat-trick. Harrow turned up with only nine men and the Reds (they played in these colours at the time) showed them no mercy.

Fulham beat Wellingborough 12–0 in a Southern League encounter in 1904, 'Boro playing so poorly that the local reporter who covered the game said that it was embarrassing to watch such incompetence from the opposition. Fulham's goalscorers were all Scottish with Alex Fraser getting 5, Willie Wardrope a hat-trick, Billy Goldie a brace, and Willie Lennie and Billy Morrison the others.

GREAT DANES

On 28 October 1908, Nils Middelboe known as the 'Great Dane' played at centre-half for the Danish amateur international side that lost 6–3 to Fulham's reserves before a crowd of 4,000. Nils gained 13 full caps for Denmark and later appeared for Chelsea. Fulham took the lead when Fred Mouncher centred but a defender kicked the ball straight at Bob Carter and the rebound flew into the net. Joe Bradshaw's shot went in off the crossbar for the second and Walter Freeman hit in an accurate drive to put Fulham three up at half time. Mouncher added an easy fourth but an own goal put Denmark on the score sheet. Freeman hit the fifth with a low scorching shot and Mouncher centred for Freeman to shoot home the sixth in between two more goals from the Danes.

FIRST TRAVEL ABROAD

Fulham played their first ever match outside of England on 27 May 1907 when they lost 2–1 to Tottenham Hotspur in friendly match in Ostend, Belgium. Five years later the Lilliewhites visited Paris on 5 May 1912 to play local rivals Queens Park Rangers in the Dubonnet Cup and won 4–1 before a crowd of 6,000. Photos still exist of this match found in a French magazine of the time.

RECORD DEFEAT IN FA CUP SEMI-FINALS

Newcastle United beat Fulham by a record 6–0 in the semi-final of the FA Cup in 1908. The match took place at Anfield and there was only a small contingent of Londoners present owing to the high prices charged by the railway companies to get to Liverpool. Regular winger Fred Threlfall was ruled out with an injury just before the match and was replaced by the inexperienced Jimmy Hogan who subsequently had a poor game. He was not alone as the form that had helped the Cottagers beat the two big Manchester clubs in earlier rounds was missing from this encounter. Fulham keeper Leslie Skene also received a serious injury during the game but carried on manfully and was a hero despite letting in 6 goals. Bill Appleyard and Jock Rutherford were the main instigators of Fulham's downfall. Appleyard scored the first and made the second for Howie. Gardner scored a soft third goal just after half time and Rutherford scored another couple before Howie slotted home once more to give the Magpies an emphatic victory. The crowd of 45,000 paid receipts of £1,700. Newcastle went on to lose to Wolves 3–1 in the final at the old Crystal Palace ground.

ALBERT WILKES TO THE RESCUE!

Albert Wilkes, the former Aston Villa, Fulham and England player, was acclaimed as a hero after rescuing a boy from drowning after he had fallen into Dartmouth Lake while playing on the ice. The *Birmingham Evening Despatch* reported that a plucky rescue from drowning was effected in Dartmouth Park, West Bromwich, by the famous footballer Albert Wilkes. It appears a number of lads had been playing upon the ice on the large boating lake. Wilkes warned them of the dangers and was walking away when he heard shouts; he ran back and found a boy named Voyse had fallen into the water. Wilkes had to break his way through the ice until he reached the place where the boy had disappeared. After some difficulty he got hold of the boy and took him to an island where he managed to revive the unconscious lad before bringing him back to the shore by boat. Wilkes sustained several cuts to his face and hands while breaking the ice but happily the lad soon made a full recovery.

LONDON CHALLENGE CUP

Fulham competed in the London Challenge Cup from 1908 to 1973. It was a very important competition when it began but by the late 1920s it had started to lose its shine and had become a competition for London reserve sides from 1931. These matches were usually played on autumn and winter Monday afternoons, which did not help attendances. Fulham competed in its inaugural season (1908/09) and lost their first tie to Woolwich Arsenal 1–0 on 28 September 1908 before a Craven Cottage crowd of 7,000.

Fulham won the London Challenge Cup in its second season – a resounding 4–0 victory over Clapton Orient at the Cottage in the first round came about with goals from Harry Brown (2), Dick Prout and Bob Dalrymple before a crowd of just 2,870. Southern Leaguers Leyton were beaten 2–1 in the next round, with two goals from Dalrymple which took the club into the semi-finals, where West Ham United were their opponents at White Hart Lane. Fred Maven and Fred Harrison were the goalscorers in a 2–1 victory before a crowd of 5,000. The final was played on 6 December 1909 at Stamford Bridge with Tottenham Hotspur the opponents. An excellent crowd of 20,000 paid receipts of £425, and saw the Cottagers earn an emphatic 4–1 victory. Dalrymple scored the first goal with a fine shot – when Robbie received the ball Darnell covered him, but after a finely judged feint, he lost the defender and shot in from 20 yards, easily beating Spurs' keeper Boreham. Dalrymple set up Harrison for the second goal when Wilkes should have cut out the pass, Harrison scoring easily. Dalrymple scored the third when he shot home after Walker's initial effort had rebounded to him. Minter obtained Spurs' solitary goal before Wilkes again made a mistake, failing to tackle Walker who passed the ball gently to Harrison to score the fourth.

ANOTHER FINAL WITH SPURS

Fulham again reached the final of the London Challenge Cup in 1910/11. The Cottagers hammered Nunhead (an Isthmian League side which went out of existence during the Second World War) 10–0 with Robert Dalrymple hitting 4 and Jimmy Torrance and Fred Harrison adding hat-tricks. The Bees were narrowly beaten 2–1 in the next round with Dalrymple and Fred Maven on target before a semi-final tie with West Ham. Willie Walker hit the winner in the second half to put the Cottagers into the final where Spurs were once again the opponents, but Tottenham got their revenge for the previous year's defeat by winning 2–1 before a 10,000 crowd at Stamford Bridge. The match was played on a cold Monday afternoon in December, thus the relatively sparse crowd.

SECRETARY TO THE QUEEN

Walter Louis Miecznikowski made his Fulham debut at Wellingborough in late December 1903, a game which the Lilliewhites won 3–2. His family came from Warsaw in Poland in the mid-nineteenth century and he attended Framlingham College in Suffolk and played for them in the final of the Suffolk Senior Cup in the 1890s. He appeared for Clapton in the final of the London Senior Cup and also played in an England amateur international trial match for the South versus the North.

Walter was awarded his London Cap & Badge while with Clapton. He then played five games for Pompey and three for the Hammers before signing for Fulham in December 1903. He remained an amateur until joining Southern United after leaving Fulham in August 1904. Walter also played 2nd XI cricket for Middlesex. He was private secretary to Queen Alexandra in 1908 and was a company director by 1933. Queen Alexandra was the consort of Edward VII who was king of England from 1901 to 1911 and her principal residences were Marlborough House, London, and Sandringham House, Norfolk, in addition to Buckingham Palace and Windsor Castle. Miecznikowski changed his name by deed poll in 1920 to plain Walter Louis.

SOUTH EASTERN LEAGUE

Fulham reserves entered the South Eastern League in 1907/08, which was a mix of league reserve teams and southern semi-professional sides such as Tunbridge Wells Rangers. The first game in September 1907 was a 2–2 draw at Stamford Bridge with Chelsea, both Fulham goals being scored by Thomas Walker who had arrived at the club from West Stanley the previous May. Fulham's biggest win in the competition was 11–1 against Bristol City in September 1911 at the Cottage with 7 goals from David Duncan plus 2 each from Arthur

Wood and Jimmy Torrance. The Lilliewhites were champions of the South Eastern League in 1914/15 but joined the London Combination after the First World War.

ARMY BAND MASTER

Wing Commander Rudolph Peter O'Donnell, a former Fulham goalkeeper (he joined on loan from Reading and played 3 times over the Christmas period in 1910/11 as regular keepers Les Skene and Jack Fryer were both injured), persuaded his bosses that great music would boost the morale of servicemen and civilians during the Second World War, and then enlisted top-notch performers. He recruited so many, in fact, that no orchestra of the time could ever have afforded to get them to perform together. Among the best of them, though only a teenager when he was called up, was horn player Dennis Brain, but other starry names included flautist Gareth Morris, violinist David Martin and the conductor Norman Del Mar. Based at Uxbridge, the orchestra was asked to play at Downing Street, tour the States and perform at the Potsdam Conference. The troops were not always so keen to hear them, however, and a former colleague quipped that they had to be marched in manacles to hear them play.

Rudy O'Donnell, Irish by descent, was one of three brothers who were all, at one time or another service bandmasters; each of them in fact served at least some time in the Royal Marines. Rudolph, the third brother, was Bandmaster to the 7th Hussars then directed the Royal Marine Artillery Band and the Portsmouth Division between 1919 and 1931 before finally transferring to the RAF (he is thought to be a unique example of a Bandmaster/Musical Director serving in all three services). O'Donnell composed the 'Celtic waltz' and a 'Fanfare on the RAF March Past'.

BROTHERS

In the early years of the club many brothers played for Fulham including Fred and Harry Spackman who had joined the club at the turn of the twentieth century. Fred Spackman was an all-round sportsmen who won prizes at sculling, swimming, gymnastics, running and skating. He played at left-half, inside left and outside left for the Cottagers and in 1902/03 won a Southern League Second Division medal. His brother Harry was a full-back who appeared for Fulham from September 1899 until he had to retire through injury in 1902. He made a total of 50 appearances for Fulham and won a Southern League Second Division championship medal in 1901/02.

Three Farnfield brothers appeared for Fulham in a Southern League encounter with West Ham United in April 1904. These were Gilbert, Herbert and Percy Farnfield who, with three of their other brothers, played in a FA Cup tie for the New Crusaders versus Plymouth Argyle but lost 6–3 in January 1906. New Crusaders were a club formed and run by the Farnfield family, which had quite a lot of success before the First World War. One of only two vicars to play for Fulham (the other was the Gilbert Montague Hall, a curate of St John's Church, Walham Green in the 1890s and later vicar at Bushey near Watford), Herbert Farnfield was vicar at St John's, Highbury (1908–11), Holy Trinity, Twickenham (1911–14), Northwood (1917–22) and chaplain at Mount Vernon Hospital from 1918 to 1922. Percy Farnfield played one first-class cricket match for Worcestershire CCC at the age of 44. Another brother Eric also appeared for Fulham in wartime football in season 1918/19 and gained an England amateur cap against France in May 1921, scoring in a 2–1 defeat at the Pershing Stadium in Paris.

Other brothers to play for Fulham are Joe and Will Bradshaw in the 1900s (their father Harry managed the club). In fact, Joe and Harry Bradshaw were the first father and son to manage Fulham during separate periods. Joe made his debut for Fulham in the same match as his brother Will in December 1904, having followed their father from Woolwich Arsenal to Fulham when he became manager of the Lilliewhites. Joe later managed Southend United, Swansea Town, Fulham and Bristol City. A quite skilful winger, Will Bradshaw had few opportunities to shine at the Cottage but played in Fulham's all-conquering reserve team of season 1904/05 which won the London League Premier and Southern League Division Two. Will later played for Burton United, Burnley and Chester after leaving the Cottage.

RUMPOLE OF THE COTTAGE

Arthur Berry, who had played for Fulham from September 1909 to February 1910, was no ordinary footballer as he was also a law student and became a well-known barrister at the Old Bailey and the Royal Courts of Justice. Arthur was one of the best amateur wingers of his time – a direct player with few thrills, he decided to join Everton when James Smith kept him out of the Fulham side. Berry gained 27 amateur caps in all, and one full cap while studying at Oxford University. He played for Oxford City against South Bank in the final of the 1913 FA Amateur Cup final.

EGYPTIAN INFLUENCE

Mohammed Al Fayed is not the first Egyptian to be associated with Fulham. Back in October 1911, they signed a player named Hassan Hegazi, 'Heggy' to his friends, from Dulwich Hamlet. Heggy, who was born in Cairo, was studying at St Catharine's College, Cambridge and playing as an amateur. He scored in his debut against Stockport County in a 3–1 victory on 11 November 1911. However, this was to be his only game for Fulham – the club wanted to sign him permanently but Hegazi wished to remain free to play for whoever he wished and decided to return to Dulwich Hamlet. He won a Cambridge Blue when he played for Cambridge University against Oxford University in February 1914 at the Queens Club and also gained his Cap & Badge for representing London. Hegazi signed for Millwall in September 1912 but never played in their first team. He returned to Egypt at the start of the First World War signing for Sekka and later appearing for Egyptian clubs Al Ahly and El Zamalek before retiring in 1931.

SKENE RETURNS

Irish side Glentoran were the visitors for a midweek friendly match on 21 March 1913. Fulham and the Belfast-based side had been in dispute over the transfer of Scottish goalkeeper Leslie Skene a few years before. Due to playing in the Irish League, Glentoran were able to sign Skene for nothing, as there was no transfer agreement between the two Football Associations, but this match was probably arranged to offer Fulham some sort of compensation. Fred Harrison scored both of Fulham's goals in a 2–0 victory but the match was abandoned after 80 minutes owing to darkness.

The first Scottish League visitors were Glasgow Rangers who beat Fulham 1–0 at the Cottage on Christmas Day 1907 before a crowd of 7,000. The Fulham team was: Crossthwaite; Ross, Charlton; Wilkes, Morrison, Hind; Hogan, McCourt, Hubbard, Fraser, Lee.

OLYMPIC GAMES

Arthur Berry won football Olympic Gold medals in 1908 and 1912. England beat Denmark 2–0 in the final at the White City, West London, in October 1908, before a crowd of 8,000. Berry won gold again in the 1912 Olympics along with other Fulham players Gordon Hoare and Harry Littlewort. This time they beat the Danes 4–2 in the final with goals from Hoare (2), Berry and Harry Walden of Bradford City.

Bernard Joy and Maurice Edelston played in the first-ever Great Britain side who appeared in the 1936 Olympics in

Berlin, but lost in the second round to Poland 5–4. Bobby Brown represented the Great Britain side in the 1960 Olympics while with Barnet and he joined Fulham as an amateur centre forward soon afterwards.

BOXERS

William Barton joined Fulham from Wandsworth FC in the summer of 1908. He usually played at right-back but played the occasional game at inside right. He never played for the Fulham first team but often appeared for the reserves and once hit two goals in a South Eastern League match at Hastings & St Leonards on 8 January 1910. Billy moved to Plymouth Argyle in the close season of 1910 and played in the first game of the season in a 0–0 draw at Portsmouth on 3 September 1910 but never appeared in their first XI again. Barton was killed in action at Pas de Calais, 8 December 1918, at the age of 33.

This is what the Fulham handbook for 1909/10 had to say about Bill Barton.

> His real name is William, but to call him so is to hide him, for though few know William Barton, everybody knows Bill as better known in the boxing ring than on the football field, he has had a wonderfully successful time as an amateur, winning competitions galore, not to mention a silver cup and a gold watch. Now he boxes professionally. As a footballer he has been associated with Willesden Town and Wandsworth. He plays the game with his whole heart. A total abstainer.

Bombardier Billy Wells played for Fulham in a number of friendlies before the First World War. He was British and British Empire Champion from 1911 until 1919, defending his title fourteen times. He became the first heavyweight to win the Lonsdale Belt in 1911, which had been introduced for British champions at all weights in 1909. Wells later became famous as the first person to be seen striking the gong in the introduction to J. Arthur Rank films. Tommy Laws who played at either right-back or right-half for Fulham in 1913/14 later recalled a friendly match at Stamford Bridge in January 1914, in which Wells made an appearance for Fulham. Tommy tackled a Chelsea player heavily and was surrounded by a number of irate opposition players. He was only 5ft 5in and was relieved when Wells came to his rescue.

EMBARRASSING SEMI-FINAL DEFEAT

The highlight of the 1911/12 London Challenge Cup competition for Fulham was David Duncan's hat-trick in a 5–2 victory over the Hammers in a first round replay. However, Fulham lost 3–1 in the next round at Clapton Orient with Scotsmen Willie Borland and Willie McIntosh making rare appearances for the first team (often first team players had not recovered from their exertions the previous Saturday so reserves were drafted into the side).

The second round tie with Orient the following season had to be replayed when it was discovered that Tom Fitchie had not been registered as a Fulham player for the required seven days. Fulham won both games comfortably 2–0 and 3–0. However, this was followed by an embarrassing 5–0 semi-final defeat against Southern League Crystal Palace at Chelsea's ground, despite fielding a strong team.

War was raging in Europe when Fulham met Brentford in September 1914 and lost 1–0. Ted Thompson made one his few appearances for the Whites at left-half before being killed in action.

LEAGUE CARRIES ON DESPITE WAR

Despite the outbreak of the First World War, league football carried on as before although there was much protest from some sections of the media who felt football should shut down for the duration. As the season developed, attendances began to drop alarmingly as more and more young men were sent to France and Belgium with the armed forces. Some of the Fulham players joined up straight away. Tommy Laws and Percy Champion had been career soldiers before joining Fulham and they soon re-enlisted, and William Garvey joined up after being released by Fulham. Ernie Coquet joined the Footballers' Battalion (1st Middlesex Regiment) and many other Fulham players returned to previous occupations such as Jimmy Torrance who became a ship boilermaker and Tom Winship who returned to Tyneside to build ships.

CROYDON COMMON

Southern League club Croydon Common made their first and last visit to Craven Cottage on 27 November 1915. The match was a London Combination fixture in a wartime competition, Fulham winning 2–0 on a frostbound pitch, which was shrouded with fog, in front of fewer than 2,000 spectators. The goals were scored in the first half by a guest player, Private 'Paddy' Allen from Clyde, despite his having played in a regimental cup final the day before. After a hand ball by Hunter, Allen secured the ball from a free kick and found the net with a powerful shot. He added the second soon afterwards, while Harry Russell later had his penalty saved by keeper Ernie Williamson after a foul on Will Taylor. Fulham had veteran Mark Bell at right-back who had played for the club from 1904 to 1907.

Croydon Common played their home matches at the Nest, which was next to Selhurst station where the railway depot now stands. The club left the London Combination in August 1916 and were wound-up the following February.

KILLED IN ACTION – FIRST WORLD WAR

Many Fulham-connected players lost their lives during the First World War. The first to be killed in action was William Borland who died at the Battle of Loos on 25 September 1915 at the age of 27. He had joined the Queen's Cameron Highlanders in October 1914 and went to France and Flanders with the expeditionary force. He is commemorated at the Loos Memorial at Pas de Calais.

Two players (Maughan and Robotham) died at the Battle of the Somme. William Maughan had broken into the Fulham team in March 1914 and looked to have an excellent career ahead of him but died on 2 October 1916. He was a corporal in the Durham Light Infantry and was buried at Dernancourt Communal Cemetery. Harry Robotham, who had played for Fulham from 1903 to 1905, enlisted at Wolverhampton and joined the Footballers' Battalion (the 1st Middlesex Regiment) but died of wounds on 12 September 1915 and is commemorated at the Thiepval Memorial.

Pint-sized Fulham and Arsenal inside forward Pat Flanagan had worked in munitions at Woolwich Arsenal until he enlisted with the Army Service Corps at Plumstead. However, he died from dysentery at the Mingoyo Clearing Station near Dar Es Salaam in German East Africa (which is now Tanzania) on 31 August 1917.

Second Lieutenant Fred Wheatcroft of the East Surrey Regiment died leading his men into action near Anneux in Northern France on 26 November 1917. He had been a schoolteacher and footballer with Fulham until 1907 and also appeared for Derby County and Swindon Town. Fred was buried in the British Cemetery at Anneux and a memorial to him was placed in his local church at Alfreton.

Arguably the most unfortunate soldiers were those who perished just before the Armistice. The young Edward Thompson (aged 24), who played just once for Fulham's league side in 1914/15, was killed in action on 6 November 1918, five days before the end of the war. Two others who died close to the end of the war were 41-year-old Fred Waterson who died on 12 October 1918 and Bob Suart who was killed on 27 September 1918. Corporal Fred Waterson, who appeared for Fulham between 1903 and 1909, died of wounds at Hazebrouck and is buried at the La Kreule British Cemetery. Suart was in the Royal Warwickshire Regiment. He was a centre-half for Fulham from 1908 until 1911 and was killed in the final push for victory.

VICTORY CUP

Fulham reached the final of the prestigious Victory Cup held in 1919 to celebrate defeating Germany in the First World War. The Munitions League were beaten 3–0 in round one with a weakened side before 3,000 spectators. Fulham took the scalp of Arsenal in the next round with a 4–1 victory at Highbury in front of 22,000, George Elliott (2), Bob Whittingham and Johnny McIntyre scoring the goals. Spurs were conquered in the semi-final with Whittingham scoring both goals in a 2–0 success with 45,000 spectating, and the final at Highbury was against Chelsea. Sadly, Fulham lost the encounter 3–0 in front of a crowd of 36,000. Fulham's team had five home-grown players in Ted Charlton, Harry Russell, Jimmy Torrance, Johnny McIntyre and Frank Penn as well as six guest players.

BROMLEY EASILY BEATEN

The London Challenge Cup returned after a four-year gap in 1919 when Fulham played Athenian League club Bromley and beat them 8–0 at Craven Cottage with goals from George Martin (3), Wattie White (3) and Donald Cock (2). The Whites beat the Gunners in the next round with an excellent 3–1 victory at Highbury, a good crowd of 10,000 seeing Cock score twice and Frank Penn add a third. However, Fulham lost to Crystal Palace 3–1 in the semi-final.

MORSE LOSES HIS ARM

In 1924/25, three players were injured when the coach in which they were travelling overturned on the way to a London Cup tie with Spurs. The Fulham trainer Elijah Morse lost his arm in the accident and was later paid significant compensation by the club after a courtroom settlement. John Brooks, the Fulham full-back, later won a bravery medal for giving blood on the spot to keep Morse alive. Not surprisingly, Fulham lost this game 5–1 with a weakened and upset side. Amazingly, there were no thoughts of postponing the match. Crowds had really dipped for London Challenge Cup games by this time and only 3,558 spectators attended the match.

ROYALTY

As far as is known no British royalty has watched a match at Craven Cottage. However, the Prince of Wales, later Edward VIII, saw Fulham play Tottenham Hotspur in a charity match at the Sandhurst Royal Military College in May 1921, with Spurs winning the game 4–0. There are photographs of the prince being presented to the Fulham team and kicking a ball next to Fulham player Donald Cock.

TRAGIC FULHAM DEATH

Inside left, Harvey Darvill died on 26 November 1924, days after playing in a match with Coventry City in which Bill Prouse scored both goals in a 2–0 victory. After returning to his home in Watford after the match, Darvill complained of stomach pains and was admitted to hospital. He died of a burst blood vessel in his stomach and there was a suspicion that the malaria that he had caught while serving in the Far East during the First World War had contributed to his death. The injury may have happened in an earlier match without him realising how serious it had been. He was buried at Watford the following Monday, on the morning of a match with Middlesbrough. A testimonial for his dependants was arranged in April 1926 but bad weather and a midweek afternoon kick-off meant that fewer than 1,000 spectators attended the game.

FULHAM'S FIRST GREAT CHAIRMAN

On 31 August 1925, John Dean became the chairman of Fulham Football Club for the second time – the first of three generations of Deans on the board. He initially became the chairman when the club became a limited company in 1903, but left the board in 1910 after a row with Henry Norris, albeit returning as a director in December 1920. When he took over, Fulham had lost £5,829 in the financial year 1924/25 – £750 for new baths, £1,000 to departing manager Phil Kelso, £1,800 in benefits to players, and a £2,500 loss on the transfer market. Dean ran a firm making household and office blinds, and he employed many Fulham players after their playing careers had ended. A benevolent man who cared greatly about the club, he died in 1944 at the age of 76.

FINANCES 1928 STYLE

Fulham were relegated to the Third Division for the first time in 1928. However, the club managed to make a profit of £2,705 over the financial year of 1927/28. Fulham took £27,517 in gate money plus £329 from season ticket sales and they also made £818 from programme sales. Their main expense, as it is today, was the player's wages, which came to £12,754, an average of £425 per player (Fulham had 30 professionals on the staff). Other outgoings were £3,428 in entertainment tax, £1,429 on hotels and travelling and £103 on the upkeep of the ground, a deficit of £2,750 in transfer fees and only £148 in player bonuses. This was a reflection of how poorly the team was doing. Shortly after

Fulham's relegation Sid Elliot, who scored 26 goals during the 1927/28 season, was sold to Chelsea for £3,600. Fulham had some disastrous buys during the year. The worst were Jack Hebden and George Horler who arrived from West Ham for a combined fee of £1,450. They were so bad that the fans nicknamed them Elsie and Doris Walters (a famous music hall act of the time).

FULHAM'S LONG-LIVING PLAYERS

Fulham's longest-living player was Wilf Nixon who died at the age of 102 at his home in Gateshead on 8 April 1985. He was a goalkeeper who was mainly reserve to Arthur Reynolds during his 12 years at Fulham. He played just 29 games for the club but was away on active service for much of the First World War. He had lied about his age when he joined the club telling them that he was 23 when in actual fact he was almost 28. Wilf played his last game for Fulham at South Shields in April 1921 at the age of 38. He was a well-built keeper with a safe pair of hands who was reliable rather than spectacular and, but for the presence of the great Arthur Reynolds, would have played many more times for Fulham. The club invited him back to Craven Cottage on his 100th birthday but unfortunately he was taken ill when a fish bone got stuck in his throat.

Close behind Nixon was John Houghton who appeared twice for Fulham in 1919. He lived until the age of 99 when he died in La Mesa, California, on 14 January 1991. He emigrated to the USA with his family, initially settling in Chicago and later worked as a production manager in Montreal and Niagara Falls. At the time of his death he'd been married for 75 years, and had three sons living in Canada and two daughters in the USA. He also had 15 grandchildren and 18 great grandchildren.

THE CARDIFF CASANOVA

Harry 'Abe' Morris and Johnny McIntyre were both on the receiving end of the wrath of Fulham's Scottish manager Phil Kelso who released these players after alleged disciplinary issues. Kelso would not tolerate a lack of discipline from his players and released them despite both looking to have great futures at the club. The first to go was Scotsman Johnny McIntyre who was transfer-listed after being caught out late before a game at Blackpool along with a number of other players. He eventually went to live close to the area so must have developed a liking for it. The other players got away with it but McIntyre also told Kelso what he thought of his managerial abilities – or lack of them – and he was on his way.

The next player to be on the receiving end of Kelso's anger was up-and-coming centre forward Harry Morris. Cardiff police saw a mystery man climb out of Morris' hotel window, walk along a narrow ledge, and enter another bedroom occupied by two nurses. There was no proof that 'Abe' was the man but he was dubbed the 'Cardiff Casanova' by the press and Kelso told him to find another club. Morris went on to become a prolific goalscorer with Brentford, Millwall, Swansea Town, Swindon Town and Clapton Orient, hitting

308 goals in 448 league and cup appearances. McIntyre also went on to better things and once scored 4 goals in 5 minutes for Blackburn Rovers against Everton in 1922/23 as well as giving Rovers and Sheffield Wednesday excellent service.

CLEAN SHEETS

Jack Fryer holds the record for the most clean sheets in consecutive matches with 7. These were the last three games of 1905/06 and the first four of 1906/07. Three matches of 1905/06 were all won 1–0 against QPR, Bristol Rovers and New Brompton before Fulham began the 1906/07 season with two 0–0 draws with Norwich City and Luton Town followed by a 3–0 victory over Crystal Palace and 1–0 success over Brentford. However, Fryer then conceded 5 goals at Spurs.

Arthur Reynolds has twice had 6 clean sheets on the trot, in 1921/22 and 1922/23. From 21 January to 6 March 1922 he did not concede a goal against Barnsley, Wolves twice, Nottingham Forest twice and Bristol City, and from 3–31 March 1923 he repeated the feat against Clapton Orient and Stockport County twice and also against Leicester City and Leeds United.

Maik Taylor managed 5 in the club's 1998/99 Third Division championship season, from 16 March to 13 April 1999 against Stoke, Blackpool, Reading, Wigan and Gillingham. Northern Ireland custodian Maik Taylor also holds the record for clean sheets in a season for Fulham with 24 during 1998/99. He was ever-present during the club's Second Division championship season, appearing in all 46 games. He beat the existing record of 18 that was held by Arthur Reynolds from as far back as 1922/23 when only 42 games were played. Taylor also kept 18 clean sheets during the 2000/01 First Division-winning season.

TRAVERS BANNED FOR LIFE

Fulham's star centre forward Barney Travers was banned for life after being found guilty of offering South Shields full-back Maitland a bribe to lose their encounter with Fulham on 18 March 1922. He found out his fate on the way to an away match with Port Vale on 1 April. Barney was the recipient of much sympathy from his team-mates and it was never proved that Fulham's manager Phil Kelso and directors of the club were involved even though it was very likely that they were. The editorial of the match programme for 17 April blamed it all on Travers, 'We are sorry for Travers because we had faith in him though any wrong doing cannot be tolerated in any form. There was no charge against us as a club, and we would like to take this opportunity of assuring our patrons that whatever happened in connection with the game in question we had no knowledge of, nor should we countenance same in the slightest degree.' This statement was not universally believed at the time but Travers was the only one ever charged with an offence. He tried to play again in Spain and Austria but was soon found out and he returned to England to run a fruit and vegetable stall in Sunderland until his death in 1955. Fulham's punishment was that they lost the record £3,000 that had been paid for his transfer.

CRICKETERS

John Arnold, Andy Ducat and Fulham reserves Percy Fender, Laurie Fishlock and Fred Durston all played for the England Test side. Ducat and Arnold gained only one cap each, Ducat against the Australians in 1921 and Arnold against New Zealand in 1931. Goalkeeper Percy Fender appeared for Fulham reserves in the early 1920s and played in 13 Tests for his country. Laurie Fishlock was another reserve who joined Fulham briefly in September 1937 after appearing for Crystal Palace, Aldershot and Millwall, and played in four Tests. Reserve goalkeeper Fred Durston, who signed for Fulham from Northfleet United in November 1922, also played in one Test and appeared regularly in county cricket for Middlesex.

Fulham first team players who also appeared in county cricket were Gordon Brice, Bill Caesar, George Cox, Percy Farnfield, Bob Gregory, Jim Hammond, Alf Pilkington and Bert White. They all played before the Second World War except Brice who appeared for Northamptonshire from 1949 to 1952 and Bedfordshire from 1953 to 1955. John Arnold played 346 matches for Hampshire from 1929 until 1950 and from 1961 became a first class umpire. George Cox, like his father, played 448 matches for Sussex from 1931 until 1960. Andy Ducat, Bob Gregory and Alf Pilkington all played for Surrey – indeed Ducat died while batting at Lords in 1942 for a Home Guard side.

The multi-talented Jim Hammond became a first class umpire at the same time as Arnold and the two former Fulham team-mates sometimes umpired in the same matches together. Hammond played in 146 matches for Sussex between 1928 and 1946. Percy Farnfield and Bill Caesar had strange county careers, Farnfield playing one match for Warwickshire in 1925 in which he scored no runs and did not bowl and Bill Caesar played one match for Surrey in 1922 but then had to wait 24 years for his second and last match for Somerset. Bert White was the son of the Lords groundsman and appeared in 8 matches for Warwickshire in 1923.

A reserve goalkeeper called Joe Hills, who joined Fulham from Swansea Town in June 1927, played for Glamorgan in 104 matches and also played for Kent as well as umpiring at county level from 1939 until 1956, including one Test match.

Bob Gregory, a full-back, who made 38 appearances for the club between 1926 and 1928, joined Fulham as an amateur from Croydon Juniors in October 1924 and signed as a professional the following May. His best season came in 1926/27 when he replaced the injured Bert Barrett at full-back for 26 games. Gregory moved to Norwich City in October 1928 but could not break into the first team. His cricket career was much more successful as Bob appeared in 413 matches for Surrey between 1925 and 1947. He scored 19,495 runs and took 437 wickets during his career as an opening batsman and leg break bowler. His highest score came in 1938 when he hit 243 runs against Somerset at the Oval. During the winter of 1933/34, Gregory toured India and Ceylon with the MCC side but did not play Test cricket.

FULHAM GO DUTCH

Fulham have twice played the Dutch national side in the days before they became one of the great football nations. The Whites won 3–0 on 22 October 1930 at Sparta Rotterdam's ground before a crowd of 8,000. The goals came from Jim Hammond (25 minutes), Jimmy Temple (62) and Fred Avey (73). The team was Iceton; Reid, Gibbon; Oliver, Dudley, Barrett; Temple, Hammond, Avey, Griffiths and Penn. The Cottagers also played the Netherlands in Amsterdam during October 1955 but the result and details are unknown.

RECORD RESERVE WIN

Fulham's reserves pulled off a remarkable 16–1 victory over Brentford on 3 April 1930, Brentford fielding a weakened side that included only three professionals in its ranks. A number of local amateurs made up the team in this Thursday afternoon encounter. Fulham's goalscorers were Fred Avey (6), Jerry Murphy (4), George Frewin (2), Joe Proud (2), George Boland with a penalty and Jack Dudley (with a rare goal). Fulham led 7–0 at half time and won with embarrassing ease and all of them had played for or would appear in Fulham's first team except Frewin.

THE LOST LONDON DERBY

Thames were formed in 1928 and played at the West Ham Stadium at Prince Regent Road in East London. They were elected to the Football League in 1930 but owing to very poor crowds only survived for two seasons before going out of business. Fulham played them on four occasions and twice drew 0–0 at Thames before crowds of fewer than 5,000. Jim Hammond scored two hat-tricks in home encounters with Thames. His first came when Fulham beat the East Londoners 4–2 in January 1931 in front of 9,064 spectators, and the Lilliewhites humiliated them in March 1932, beating them 8–0 before 18,875 with goals from Hammond (3), Billy Richards (2), Frank Newton (2) and Jack Finch. Four players appeared for both clubs – Jack Hebden, Eddie Perry, Johnny Tonner and Bert White.

RECORD VICTORY OVER Ks

Fulham's record score in the London Challenge Cup came on 15 October 1928 when Kingstonian were beaten 11–2, with goals from Fred Avey (4), Jimmy Temple (3), Bill Haley, Harry Daykin, Bert Barrett and Johnny Price. Daykin never played in the first team again. He had been signed from Southend United and later played for Mansfield Town, Ilkeston Town, and Sutton Town. Unfortunately, the Whites lost 4–1 at the Valley in the next round. Fulham's final 'first team match' in the London Challenge Cup was a humiliating 3–1 defeat at home to non-league Ilford in October 1930. Fulham put out their reserve side for this game, which included the goalkeeper

Monty Garland-Wells for his only game in a Fulham shirt. Monty was an England amateur international who won a Blue at football and rugby while attending Pembroke College, Oxford. He also played 130 matches for Surrey's county side between 1928 and 1939 and was a hard-hitting middle order batsman and a right-arm medium pace bowler. Monty had played eleven times for Clapton Orient the previous season.

TORQUAY HIT FOR TEN

Fulham pulled off their best victory since joining the Football League in 1907 when they beat Torquay United 10–2 at Craven Cottage on a mild September evening. In a one-sided game Jim Hammond scored 4 goals, the last three being in succession. Torquay had let in 24 goals in their first four games and had a number of first team players out through injury. Fulham brought in two young wingers who excelled; Joe Proud and Jack Finch, replacing regulars Frank Penn and Billy Richards, who had a field day as they took United's defence apart. Frank 'Bonzo' Newton scored for Fulham after five minutes but a muscle injury later slowed him down. Finch scored the second after a goalmouth scramble. Proud drove in a rebound from a shot from Finch and Hammond hooked in number four, Newton and Price adding further goals to give Fulham a 6–0 interval lead. Hammond scored a soft seventh then Hutchinson pulled a goal back for Torquay. Hammond scored another after a brilliant dribble and unstoppable shot. Stabb scored United's second but Hammond was gifted the ninth and Johnny Price shot through after a scrimmage in front of the goal for Fulham's tenth goal.

THIRD DIVISION SOUTH CHAMPIONS

Fulham produced a souvenir programme for their final home game of the 1931/32 season against Exeter City on 7 May 1932. This was to commemorate the club winning the Third Division South championship that season. The programme included photos of most of the players as well as manager James McIntyre and chairman John Dean. There was a historical review of some of the great names that had played for Fulham up until that time and a review of the reserve team, which had won the London Challenge Cup by beating Crystal Palace. Eddie Perry had scored 34 goals for the reserves over the season. Mr Morton T. Cadman, a member of the Football League Management Committee, presented the championship shield to the team in the absence of its president John McKenna. Fulham beat Exeter City 3–1 thanks to goals from Jim Hammond and Frank Newton (2) before a crowd of 15,502.

RESERVES TRIUMPH AT LAST

Fulham reserves took over from the first team in 1931/32 in the London Challenge Cup competition, Charlton Athletic being beaten 5–1 in the first round with 4 goals from Eddie Perry and another from Billy Richards. Chelsea were defeated 2–0 at Stamford Bridge in round two with goals from Jerry Murphy and the veteran Frank Penn. Fulham triumphed over Millwall 2–1 in the semi-final at Stamford Bridge with goals from Perry and Joe Proud. The final was played on 9 May

1932 when Crystal Palace were beaten 2–1 at Selhurst Park with goals from Sonny Gibbon and Johnny Price. Fulham's team was: Mason; Hindson, Ford; Keen, Malkey, Webb; Proud, Perry; Gibbon, Price, Penn.

Fulham reached the final again in 1947/48 after defeating Wimbledon 4–1 at Plough Lane in the first round and Dulwich Hamlet 4–0 at home in the second round with goals from John Jones, Cyril Grant, Dave Bewley and Syd Thomas. Millwall were again the Whites' semi-final opponents and were beaten 4–2 at the Cottage with goals from Grant, Ayres, J. Jones and an own goal. On 19 April 1948, however, Tottenham Hotspur were successful in the final with a 3–1 victory with Wally Hinshelwood hit Fulham's consolation goal.

Fulham won the London Challenge Cup again in 1951/52 beating Charlton Athletic in the Final 1–0 on 10 December 1951 at Stamford Bridge, Wally Hinshelwood this time scoring the winner. They had beaten Wimbledon 5–1, Finchley 2–1 in a replay (after a 2–2 draw) and Millwall 2–1 after another 2–2 draw in the semi-final with Reg Lowe scoring with a header from 60 yards.

GOALS, GOALS, GOALS!

Frank 'Bonzo' Newton holds the record for goals in consecutive matches with 13 in 9 games during 1932/33 from 15 October to 10 December. He hit 2 against Lincoln, Burnley, Bradford Park Avenue and Plymouth in consecutive matches then one against Oldham, Manchester United, Stoke, Charlton and Tottenham Hotspur in the next 5 games.

The most explosive start to a season was when Ronnie Rooke began the 1944/45 season with 15 goals in the first 5 games, his sequence being Chelsea (4), Reading (2), QPR (1), Brighton (4) and Crystal Palace (4). That season he hit 27 goals in just 15 appearances, also spending a great deal of time serving his country in the war in Italy.

BONZO'S FINALE

The Fulham manager, Jimmy Hogan, arranged a match with one of his former clubs, FK Austria, the game kicking off at 2.30 p.m. on Monday 3 December 1934. This match was to be the last for the Cottagers' centre forward Frank 'Bonzo' Newton. Unfortunately, he broke his leg and was replaced by Eddie Perry for the second half, one of the first substitutions of a Fulham player. The following programme stated that Frank remained in hospital due to complications from his broken leg and put the injury down to an unfortunate accident. The game ended in an entertaining 1–1 draw with Jim Hammond scoring a late equaliser for Fulham.

JIMMY HOGAN SACKED IN HOSPITAL

Fulham appointed Jimmy Hogan as manager during the summer of 1934, a former player who had become a famous coach on the continent since leaving the club. He had coached in Hungary, Germany, Holland, Switzerland

and Austria, including taking charge of international sides. Indeed, he was the coach of Austria when they narrowly lost to England at Highbury in 1932 and came to Fulham with an excellent reputation. However, Hogan did not last long as Fulham's manager, being sacked in February 1935 after indifferent results and while in hospital recovering from an operation.

TRAGIC DEATH OF SONNY

Everybody who played or worked for Fulham was in a state, of shock after the untimely death of the very popular full-back Samuel 'Sonny' Gibbon on 8 April 1935 at the young age of 25. Sonny was returning to London on his motorbike with a pillion passenger when, soon after leaving Deal in Kent, he crashed into a car and was instantly killed and his friend badly injured. He was buried in his hometown of Merthyr Tydfil and many of his team-mates attended the funeral the day after losing 2–0 at Swansea Town. He was the son of Merthyr Town's chairman and had been sold to the Whites to prevent the club from going bankrupt. Gibbon had played 127 first team games for Fulham at the time of his death.

DEBUTANT SCORERS

Two players have hit hat-tricks on their debut for Fulham: Ronnie Rooke, who had been signed from Crystal Palace, scored 3 against West Ham United at the Cottage in November

1936 and Doug McGibbon repeated this feat in January 1947. He scored a hat-trick against Plymouth Argyle after his arrival from Bournemouth for an £8,000 fee.

BIGGEST CROWD AT THE COTTAGE

The biggest crowd ever at Craven Cottage of 49,335 attended a game with Millwall on 8 October 1938. This beat the previous record of 43,407 set in 1933 against Spurs. This was the first home game after Neville Chamberlain, the British Prime Minister, returned from signing the Munich Pact with Hitler and the population was celebrating as it looked as though war had been prevented. Both sides were in the top three in the Second Division and the crowd was 10,000 greater than at any other ground in the country that day. Many crash barriers collapsed and later the club had to strengthen every barrier on the ground owing to safety concerns. Millwall took the lead when Mike Keeping deflected Barker's shot past his own keeper. After the break Fulham equalised when Arnold sent in a perfect free kick for Viv Woodward to head home. The winning goal for Fulham came after Ronnie Rooke was fouled, Jim Evans touching home Johnny Arnold's free kick.

FIRST WARTIME MATCH AT THE COTTAGE

The first match to be played at Craven Cottage after the outbreak of the Second World War came when Portsmouth visited on 29 October 1939. The Home Office had closed

Craven Cottage immediately following the commencement of hostilities in early September. A number of friendlies were played on opponents' grounds but, with the commencement of regional competitions, games were again played at Fulham's ground, although the Home Office set a crowd limit of only 8,000. Jim Tompkins, Harry Freeman and Sam Malpass joined the Army immediately and Tompkins had his first stripe by November, being promoted to corporal. Eddie Perry became a sergeant with the Army Physical Training School at Aldershot and Jim Taylor and Harry Cranfield had also been called up.

Fulham beat Pompey 2–1 with goals from Ronnie Rooke before a crowd of 6,468. It was announced in the programme that in the event of an air raid the nearest public shelters were at the Recreation Ground at Fulham Palace Road and supporters could take cover under the stand. Fulham wing-half Jim Evans was sent off in a match with Brentford in December 1939 which was a rare event in those days.

FULHAM AT WAR

1941 was a grim year for London – the Germans were blitzing the capital and there were restrictions on the movements of the population. Identity cards were needed to enter certain areas and with many men and women away on active service, the crowds at Craven Cottage rarely passed the 2,000 mark. Many potential spectators also worked on Saturdays, mainly in munitions or the public services. Fulham relied on guest players to make up the numbers and these ranged from unknown amateurs who conned themselves a game to international players. It was not unknown for potential guests to introduce themselves as a pre-war player only for the club to quickly realise that they had been misled when they saw the person play, when it became obvious that they had never played at that level before. Guests in 1941 included internationals such as Sam Weaver, Harry Hobbus, Stan Cullis and Cliff Bastin the famous Arsenal left-winger. Other less well-known players included David Thomas of Plymouth Argyle, who scored 20 goals in 44 appearances for Fulham, the brother of Bob who played for Fulham at centre forward after the war. Other regulars were keepers Frank Boulton (Derby County) and Phil Joslin (Torquay United), and George Matthewson, Bury's centre-half.

LEAGUE WAR CUP RUN

Fulham reached the semi-final of the League War Cup in 1940, the equivalent of the FA Cup. The competition was packed into a seven-week period close to the end of the season. In the first round Brentford were beaten 4–1 at home with goals from David Thomas (from Plymouth Argyle), Johnny Arnold (2) and Ronnie Rooke, Fulham winning again 2–1 at Griffin Park in the second leg with goals from Viv Woodward and Len Jones. Norwich City gave the Cottagers a more difficult time in the second round but after a 1–1 draw at Carrow Road (Rooke scoring for Fulham), the Whites won the second leg 1–0 thanks to Jim McCormick's goal. Nottingham Forest were the opponents in the third round and Fulham won 2–0 at the Cottage with goals from Rooke and an own goal. People were becoming more interested in the competition and a crowd of 14,705 was present for the visit of Everton in the quarter-final where Fulham were emphatic winners by 5–2 with Woodward (2), Rooke, McCormick and Arnold on the score sheet for the Whites and Gillick and Tommy Lawton replying for the Toffees. The semi-final was played at nearby Stamford Bridge with East Londoners West Ham United the opponents. The game kicked off at 6.40 p.m. to accommodate the many war workers who wished to attend, Fulham losing the seven-goal thriller in front of a crowd of 32,799. Woodward and Rooke (2–1 a penalty) were on target for Fulham but Foxall, Goulden, Small and an own goal earned the Hammers a 4–3 victory. West Ham went on to beat Blackburn Rovers 1–0 in the final at Wembley.

DURING THE WAR . . .

Fulham players were spread far and wide in 1943 owing to the war. Sid Thomas was stationed in West Africa and played football against the locals. He described them as not knowing very much about the game but being very fast. Jimmy Hughes and Doug Flack were in India and met each other when on opposing sides in a representative match near Calcutta. Johnny Arnold had an easy war, packing cigarettes and tobacco for the troops while Bob Thomas was a naval stoker after working as a shell-loader before his call-up. Len Quested luckily spent the war sailing in a tug around Sydney

Harbour but Ernie Shepherd had a more difficult time. He was marooned in Malta during a long period when the island was bombed continuously over many weeks.

Harry Wallbanks was a miner in Northumberland and played for Sunderland, Larry Gage was a paratrooper and Corporal Viv Woodward was a lorry driver with the RAOC. Ronnie Rooke scored many goals for Fulham until his army unit was transferred to Italy where he saw active service and future Fulham manager Alec Stock became a captain and commanded a tank crew in Caen, France, where he was wounded by shrapnel in his back.

MORE WARTIME EXPERIENCES

The Second World War had ended in May 1945 but most Fulham players were still in the armed services by January 1946. Prolific goalscorer Ronnie Rooke was the first player to be demobbed that month and full-back Sam Malpass became the second player to leave the services and sign as a professional for Fulham. Sam had been stationed in India and played for touring Army Representative side there. The news reached the Cottage that goalkeeper Doug Flack had been elected to tour India with an RAF side. Reserve team player Albert Hudson returned from service in India in March 1946 and impressed with his fitness in his first game for Fulham while flying winger Arthur Stevens was demobbed in June 1946 after serving with the BAOR. Pre-war star winger Johnny Arnold announced that he was retiring from the game and was now 'mine host' at a hotel in Southampton.

His former Saints team-mate Mike Keeping took up a coaching post in Holland while youngster Dennis Rampling was actually called up in March 1946 and joined the RAF. He was stationed near Leicester and joined the RAF Physical Training staff. On 2 March 1946, Fulham played Arsenal at the Cottage and won 2–1. Oswald Evans made his debut in goal and did well 'in spite of carrying much overweight' – he reputedly weighed over 20 stone.

WARTIME INTERNATIONALS

Joe Bacuzzi appeared 13 times for England during the war years, including four matches against Scotland. He was on the winning side in three of these games but was on the losing side when England went down 5–4 at Hampden Park in April 1942. Other wartime internationals were Ronnie Rooke (one cap for England against Wales in October 1942), Eddie Perry for Wales against England in April 1941 and Viv Woodward who scored for Wales against England in a 3–2 defeat in June 1941.

JONES AT WAR

During the war season of 1944/45, Fulham used six guest players with the surname of Jones. A regular during the war years was Len Jones who scored 8 times in 118 appearances for the club. He also played for Barnsley, Plymouth Argyle,

Southend United, Colchester and Ipswich Town during his career. The other Joneses played only a handful of matches for Fulham. These were: Charlie Jones, a centre-half from Southend United; Fred Jones, a centre forward from Ipswich Town; Eric Jones, a winger with Stoke City; George Jones, an outside left from Sheffield United and Sam Jones a wing-half from Blackpool who became a Northern Irish International after the war.

WARTIME DEATHS – SECOND WORLD WAR

Five Fulham connected players died while serving their country in the Second World War. These were Dennis Higgins, George Fairbairn, Jim Tompkins, Ernie Tuckett and Jock Dodds, all of whom played for Fulham before the war.

One of the most heroic and tragic figures to play for Fulham, Jimmy Tompkins was a fine left-half. His somewhat lightweight frame was well suited to the wing-half position, and he made the breakthrough in the 1936 semi-final team. From then until the start of hostilities, the number six shirt was his own and his style was characterised by tight marking, fierce tackling and good distribution. He was cool, stylish and mature beyond his years and always the epitome of fairness. When war was declared he saw action early because of his experience with the Territorial Army. He joined the Royal Fusiliers (City of London Regiment) in 1939 and soon obtained his first stripe. By 1944 he was a major but was killed on 10 July shortly after the D-Day landings. His death is commemorated at the Bayeux Memorial, as he has no known grave.

Dennis Higgins, a red-headed direct outside right who joined Fulham in November 1935, died in Egypt on active service on 25 September 1942 aged only 26. His death is commemorated at the Alamein Memorial, which forms the entrance to the El Alamein War Cemetery. He was one of the many dead soldiers who had no known grave. He was a private with the Durham Light Infantry's 9th Battalion and left a young wife, Nancy, in his hometown of Leek. Higgins had played for Leek and Tamworth before his arrival at Craven Cottage. He scored a hat-trick for Fulham at Bradford Park Avenue in January 1939 and his career looked on the point of taking off when war was declared.

Ernie Tuckett was a corporal with the Royal Air Force Volunteer Reserve when he was killed in a flying accident in North Yorkshire on 27 May 1945. Ernie played very little football during the war and concentrated on his RAF duties. Rising to the rank of corporal, Tuckett was buried at Boosbeck (St Aidan's churchyard), Yorkshire.

A centre forward from Belfast, 'Jock' Dodds was 19 when he came to Craven Cottage from Linfield in July 1934. His only Fulham appearance came at West Ham United in April 1936. Dodds was killed in Singapore on 26 January 1942.

George Harding Fairbairn was a reserve at Fulham but was said to have a great future in football when he was killed just south of Tunis on 21 February 1943 at the age of 23. He had played as a guest for Dundee United in August 1942.

IRISH LEAGUE REPRESENTATIVES

The Irish League used to be a much stronger competition than it is today. Most good Irish players presently come to ply their trade in either the English or Scottish Leagues but in the 1940s most stayed at home. Fulham were one of the first clubs to seek talented players from Northern Ireland and in 1949 signed Robin Lawler, Johnny Campbell and Hugh Kelly from Belfast Celtic, a club that was soon to become defunct owing to the troubles in Belfast. Kelly was a well-established goalkeeper who had appeared eight times for the Irish League while Lawler had appeared in two representative matches in 1948 against the Scottish League and Campbell played four times. One of these matches was a 7–4 defeat against the Scottish League in which he scored twice in April 1947. Also in the side on this occasion were Paddy Molloy who performed for Fulham in the early 1930s and was then with Distillery, and Bobby Brennan who also later played for Fulham. Ted Hinton, a future Fulham keeper, represented the Northern Ireland Regional League against the League of Ireland in April 1942 while with Glentoran.

Three other Fulham-connected players have won Irish League representative honours – Ivan Murray, Brendan Mullan and Colin McCurdy. Murray and Mullan joined Fulham from Coleraine in 1968 but neither made much of an impact at the Cottage. Mullan represented the Irish League on two occasions and one of these was against the Football League at Norwich where they lost 5–0. Murray also played twice against the League of Ireland in 1967 and 1974. McCurdy had one game for Fulham in 1978 but played three times for the Irish League. Two of these came on a tour to

Canada in September 1980 and he scored in both games against the host nation in Newfoundland and Toronto.

MOSCOW DYNAMOS COME TO TOWN

The Russian champions Dynamo Moscow visited Britain in November 1945 and fired the imagination of a population that had been starved of entertainment during the war years. They played two matches in London against Chelsea and Arsenal, but Fulham players featured in both games. Jim Taylor and Joe Bacuzzi played for Chelsea, and Ronnie Rooke and Bacuzzi played for Arsenal. Over 100,000 people descended on Stamford Bridge for a Wednesday afternoon match – the crowd was officially 85,000 but many more broke into the ground as spectators found every vantage spot they could, hundreds even climbing onto the roof of the stand to get a better view. The teams emerged side by side and the Russian team presented the Chelsea side with flowers, which bemused the opposition players. An exciting game ended in a 3–3 draw and Taylor and Bacuzzi both had good games. The game at Highbury was played in dense fog and many of the 54,600 crowd saw very little of the game. Dynamo won in controversial circumstances 4–3, Ronnie Rooke having what looked a perfectly good goal to make the score 4–4 ruled out by the Russian referee. Arsenal also included Stanley Matthews and Stan Mortensen, the famous Blackpool pair, in their line-up. There were many controversial moments as the Russian referee seemed to lose his grip. At one time Dynamo had 12 players on the pitch and the referee sent off Arsenal's George Drury but he ignored him and stayed on.

OLDEST SURVIVING PLAYERS

Who is the oldest surviving Fulham player? At the time
of writing this book the oldest surviving player is almost
definitely Dave Bewley who was born at Christchurch,
Hampshire, on 22 September 1920. A reliable wing-half,
Dave Bewley appeared six times in Fulham's Second Division
championship side of 1948/49 and also played for Watford
and Reading. After leaving the game, Bewley worked for a
photographic company in Hemel Hempstead for 26 years
before retiring to live in Cirencester. He has been married
for 70 years and met his wife Myra, 89, at a dance in their
hometown of Bournemouth in 1939. The couple were married
in January 1941. Just one week later, Bewley joined the Royal
Artillery where he remained for the duration of the Second
World War. They raised their three children Lesley, Kevin and
Stephanie. The couple also have four grandchildren and six
great grandchildren.

Len Quested was born in Folkestone, Kent, on 9 January
1925 and currently lives in Australia. He joined Fulham
from Folkestone Town as an amateur in 1943 and turned
professional in August 1946. Len left the Cottage for
Huddersfield Town in November 1951 and he emigrated to
Australia in 1957 and in the early 1980s was reported to be a
director of a league club in that country.

Dennis Rampling was born in Gainsborough, Lincolnshire,
on 25 November 1923 and joined Fulham in November 1942
before moving on to Bournemouth & Boscombe Athletic in
July 1948. Dennis revisited the Cottage in September 1999 as
a guest of the club as a present arranged by his family.

Wally Hinshelwood is also thought to be still alive and he was born at Lambeth, London, on 27 October 1929 and joined Fulham from Sutton United in August 1945 and after a brief spell at Chelsea moved on to Reading in December 1952. His sons Paul and Martin later played for Crystal Palace.

THE COTTAGERS' NORTH AMERICAN TOUR

On 15 May 1951, Fulham embarked on a tour of Canada and the USA, which saw them play matches in Toronto, New York, Montreal, Edmonton, Vancouver, Victoria and Winnipeg. They sailed from. Liverpool on the SS *Empress of Scotland*. The Atlantic crossing was rough and not all of the players were good sailors, several spending much of the time in their cabins. Among the ever-presents in the dining saloon were Bob Thomas (an old sailor), Archie Macaulay, Bobby Robson, Harry Freeman, Frank Penn, Frank Osborne and manager Bill Dodgin. During the tour Fulham played Glasgow Celtic on three occasions, the clubs beating each other once and the other game was a draw. Fulham played a selection of 'all star' sides drawn from the best clubs within the Provinces that they played. It was a pleasant trip involving long journeys across thousands of miles and through magnificent scenery. In the days before air travel became the norm, the party travelled everywhere by train. They arrived back in Liverpool on 29 June 1951, most of the players having enjoyed a never-to-be-forgotten experience.

FULHAM'S GOLDEN VOICE

Jeff Taylor joined Fulham from Huddersfield Town in a player-exchange deal which saw Len Quested go in the other direction in November 1951. Scoring 30 goals in only 71 games for Huddersfield, Fulham must have felt they had signed a regular goalscorer; alas, Jeff struggled to gain a regular place in the Fulham team. However, he did score two hat-tricks for the club, against Middlesbrough in a 6–0 win in January 1952 and against Grimsby Town in a sensational FA Cup tie that finished 5–5 two years later. He gained a BA Honours degree in Geography and Geology at University College, London – funding his studies with money earned from football – and became deeply involved in music-making. He went on to study at the Royal Academy of Music and after graduating retired from football and embarked on a substantial and successful singing career under the name Neilson Taylor. An extremely versatile singer, Jeff was regarded as one of the best baritones of his generation, a world-class performer. He also had wonderful skills as a pianist, composer and later, as a teacher.

Neilson Taylor was singing at Glyndebourne when Luciano Pavarotti was starring in Mozart's opera, *Idomeneo*, and the Italian master introduced Taylor to his own voice teacher, Ettore Campogalliani. Taylor went to Milan to learn from Campogalliani and when he returned, performed at Covent Garden. Regular appearances on the BBC followed in their once-a-week opera broadcasts. One of his excellent recordings was the Verdi opera *The Sicilian Vespers*. While continuing to perform, Jeff went into teaching at the Royal Scottish Academy of Music and Drama in Glasgow, being appointed Professor of Singing in 1974.

JUNIORS

The Juniors first entered the FA Youth Cup during 1953/54 in the second year of the competition. They drew 1–1 at Hendon in their first match, winning the replay 6–0. One of Fulham's best seasons in the competition came in 1985/86 when they reached the fifth round (quarter-finals) but lost 3–0 to Manchester City at the Cottage. They had beaten Orient, Birmingham City and Mansfield Town to reach this stage. The Fulham side included six players who would perform in the Football League – Gary Smith, Shaun Gore, Glen Thomas, Justin Skinner, Kevin Hoddy and Paul Mortimer. Prior to this, Fulham had reached the fourth round twice in 1967 and 1971 but lost to West Ham United on both occasions. Fulham Juniors won the South East Counties League Cup in 1971/72 when they beat Arsenal 3–2 on aggregate over a two-legged final. The Juniors' best season in the South East Counties League came in 1954/55 when they finished as runners-up to Chelsea. This side included Tony Macedo, Trevor Watson, Derek Lampe, Brian O'Connell and Tony Barton, all of whom appeared in Fulham's first team in future years. They also beat Brentford in the final of the League Cup that season.

SOUTHERN FLOODLIT CUP

The Southern Floodlit Cup was a competition for league clubs in the southern half of England, which began in 1955/56 but Fulham did not enter the competition until 1957. The reason for this was their Craven Cottage ground did not have floodlights until the 1960s, so if there were any home matches these would have to be played elsewhere. Fulham beat Chelsea 2–1 at Stamford Bridge with goals from John Doherty and Roy Bentley before a crowd of 15,056, in their first match in the competition but lost 4–2 at Watford in the second round in front of an attendance of 4,927. The following season, Fulham beat QPR 4–0 at Loftus Road with goals from Doherty, Bentley, Johnson and Key but lost 3–1 at West Ham in the following round, watched by a meagre 4,500. 1959/60 was the last season of the competition, which was replaced by the Football League Cup. Fulham played two 'home' matches at Brentford (there are programmes for these games) and then they beat Luton Town 1–0 in a replay in late November with Tosh Chamberlain scoring the winner. However, they went out to Coventry City 1–0 in front of 4,800 fans in the next round.

SEMI-FINAL DEFEAT TO BUSBY BABES

1958 was the year of the terrible Munich air crash in which many of Manchester United's Busby Babes side lost their lives. The nation's sympathies were very much with United when they managed to fight their way to the semi-finals of the FA Cup, despite having to build a side from scratch. Fulham were on a hiding to nothing as emotions ran high at Highbury after a 2–2 draw at Villa Park had led to a replay. Tony Macedo, who had an outstanding game in the first match, had a stinker in the replay as United scored five times. The game was a close affair despite this as Dawson put United into the lead with a diving header but Arthur Stevens equalised from close range. Macedo should have saved Dawson's second which somehow slipped under his body and then Jim Langley dribbled 40 yards to give Tosh Chamberlain the chance to level the score at 2–2. Another Dawson header led to Brennan putting United ahead again, and Dawson completed his hat-trick after a great run from Bobby Charlton. Roy Dwight pulled a goal back for Fulham and then had a goal disallowed for handball before Charlton hit United's fifth just before the end.

5-A-SIDE TRIUMPH

Fulham won the Evening News Five-a-Side competition at Harringay Arena on 13 April 1955. The BBC televised the final live and Fulham's team comprised Ian Black in goal, Eddie Lowe, Jimmy Hill, Johnny Haynes and Bobby Robson. Arsenal had been beaten in the second round after extra time, the full time score being stuck at 2–2. Fulham eventually won 4–2 with goals from Hill and a Haynes hat-trick and then triumphed in their semi-final easily, dispatching Charlton 5–1 with goals from Hill, Haynes and Robson (3). Fulham went on to win the final against West Ham United 4–1; Hill scored an early goal but Parker equalised for the Hammers. Robson then scored two quick goals and Haynes added a fourth. As well as winning a cup, each player received a handsome silver medal to remember their triumph.

RECORD GOALS IN FA CUP TIE AT THE COTTAGE

One of the greatest games ever at the Cottage took place in late January 1956 when Fulham met Newcastle United in an FA Cup fourth round tie. At one point Fulham were 3–0 down but pulled back to lead 4–3 before letting in two late goals to lose 5–4. Fulham's unfortunate hero was Tosh Chamberlain who scored a hat-trick but still ended up on the losing side. The game had everything including a very controversial goal as well as Chamberlain having another goal ruled out early in the second half. United's equaliser to make it 4–4 would not be allowed today. Vic Keeble, their centre forward, barged into keeper Ian Black and sent the player and the ball over the line. Keeble then rubbed salt into the wound by scoring the winning goal, heading home with 8 minutes to go. Chamberlain's goals came in the 39th, 68th and 70th minutes. Jimmy Hill put Fulham into the lead three minutes later from close range – Fulham's third goal in five minutes – but all to no avail!

LITTLE BIRD AT THE COTTAGE

One of the greatest ever players, 'Little Bird' Garrincha was on view on the right wing for Brazilian club Botafogo on 9 April 1956. He was a very clever and tricky winger who was later to star in the 1958 and 1962 World Cup finals for Brazil. Fulham were not at full strength and had Tommy Cronin at right-half and Joe Hall at inside left. Hall scored one of the Fulham goals in a rare appearance for the club and his career was sadly ended soon afterwards by a leg injury. The 4 goals came in a 5-minute spell. Alarcon gave the Brazilians the lead in the 10th minute but Roy Dwight and Hall netted for Fulham before Garrincha equalised. The game attracted a 12,000 crowd, which was excellent considering the game kicked off at 5.30 p.m. on a Monday evening.

CLUB PRESIDENT

Sir Leslie Cecil Blackmore Bowker (KCVO OBE MC) was Fulham's club president in the early 1950s. He was a full-back who had joined Fulham from the West London Old Boys in April 1911. He left the club in 1914 to serve as a captain with the London Scottish Regiment during the First World War but then joined Dulwich Hamlet in 1919, playing in their 1920 FA Amateur Cup-winning side alongside future Fulham full-back Alf Pilkington. Other club presidents have been former chairman Tommy Trinder and Arsenal's great centre forward Ted Drake who was employed by Fulham in the 1970s to help develop players.

THE IRON MAN COMETH

As part of the Festival of Britain celebrations, Fulham entertained Dinamo of Yugoslavia at Craven Cottage on 10 May 1951. Fulham won the game 3–1 with goals from Bobby Brennan, Jimmy Bowie and Arthur Stevens. For the visit of Spartak to Craven Cottage on 28 April 1956, the opposition had a 6ft 4in centre-half called Stefanovics (spelled 'Sdafanovics' in the match day programme) who had the nickname 'The Iron Man'. Arthur Stevens scored from the edge of the box after a pass from Norman Smith to give the Whites the lead, and then Johnny Haynes made it 2–0 after a wonderful return pass from Stevens. Haynes had a fine game despite appearing for the Football League in Ireland the previous day. Roy Dwight made it 3–0 before Tikics scored a late consolation goal.

FIRST GERMAN VISITORS

Fulham met West German side Blauweiss in a match played on Saturday afternoon 27 April 1957. Fulham won easily by hitting 6 goals from Haynes (40 mins), Dwight (48, 82), Stevens (52), Bentley (51) and Chamberlain (79). The first German side to visit the Cottage, Blauweiss were completely outclassed by Fulham but managed to only concede one goal in the first half mainly due to an outstanding goalkeeping display from Wartig.

Ferencváros of Hungary were the first foreign opposition for a floodlit friendly at the Cottage on 9 December 1963. Their best players were Flórián Albert, who was to star for the Hungarians during the 1966 World Cup in England, and Dr Máté Fenyvesi who had been capped 50 times by Hungary. Graham Leggat and Johnny Key scored for Fulham and Albert hit the visitors' consolation goal.

MACEDO IS FLOWN HOME

Thanks to the kind co-operation of the Royal Air Force, Fulham were able to get Tony Macedo back from Germany where he was completing his national service. Owing to a shortage of goalkeepers, with Ken Hewkins injured, Fulham needed Tony badly for a London Challenge Cup match in October 1957. So after secretary-general manager Frank Osborne telephoned Macedo's commanding officer, the young goalkeeper was flown over from Goch near Düsseldorf and back again. The same thing happened a fortnight later for a reserve fixture with Crystal Palace. Tony's flight cost the club about £14 each time but felt it was money well spent. It was not long before Macedo had finished his national service and was a regular in the first team. Macedo was one of Fulham's best ever keepers and went on to play 391 games for the club. He could have played for England if he had been more consistent but did appear ten times for the Under-23 side. After he left Fulham, Tony played for Colchester United before moving to South Africa to play for Durban City and Highlands Park. Tony revisited Craven Cottage in August 2011 after a gap of 43 years having spent many years living in South Africa and Australia.

JOHNNY CAMPBELL

When Fulham's inside right Johnny Campbell was forced to give up the game due to illness, a testimonial game was arranged to help him with his finances. He had to face a

number of operations that year and when he walked into a
lamp post and blood gushed out of his forehead, the club's
programme stated that it was surprised and delighted he still
had some blood in his veins due to the number of operations
he had endured! After his retirement from playing, Johnny
worked for Fulham as a scout in Northern Ireland until his
untimely death in January 1968.

RECORD DEFEAT AT MOLINEUX

Fulham's record defeat in the Football League came at
Wolverhampton Wanderers' Molineux ground in September
1959, when they were hit for 9, with Norman Deeley scoring
4 of the goals. Wolves took the lead after only 6 minutes
through Deeley and they led 3–0 at the interval with the help
of a great 25-yard shot from Ron Flowers. Between the 58th
and 74th minute, Wolves hit 5 goals with the Fulham defence
reeling. Deeley made it 9 with 3 minutes to go before keeper
Tony Macedo made a great save to prevent Deeley making it
10 in the final minute. Fulham had actually beaten Wolves
3–1 the previous week at the Cottage.

ANOTHER SEMI-FINAL DEFEAT

Fulham, yet again, failed to reach the final of the FA Cup in
1962. This was the fourth time that they had lost at the semi-
final stage. The season had been spent fighting relegation

from Division One and the cup run was seen as light relief by the club's supporters who had not expected Fulham to do so well in the competition. Fulham met Burnley at Villa Park on the last day of March and they came very close to victory but drew 1–1. The replay was at Filbert Street on 9 April and again the night was to end in total disappointment. Fulham would have met Tottenham Hotspur in the final if they had won but Burnley soaked up Fulham's pressure and struck twice on the break. Jimmy McIlroy and Ray Pointer set up Harris to scoop the ball into the net past Tony Macedo after 30 minutes. It was Robson who scored again, 10 minutes from time, to give Burnley a lucky 2–0 lead. Johnny Haynes almost scored on three occasions but it was left-back Jim Langley who scored Fulham's consolation goal a minute from time. His shot from 25 yards must have deflected off three different players as it ricocheted into the net. Unfortunately, it was too late for Fulham to find an equaliser.

BOXING DAY TRIUMPH

Fulham produced their greatest league win on Boxing Day 1963 when they beat visitors Ipswich Town 10–1 – a team which had won the league championship only 18 months earlier. The match was not as one-sided as the score suggests and Town were unlucky to concede 5 goals in the second half. Every time Fulham attacked they seemed to score. Cook gave them the lead from a cross from Graham Leggat, then Leggat scored a hat-trick in only 3 minutes to equal the quickest hat-trick in Division One. His third was the best, a tremendous shot from 25 yards. Bobby Howfield made it 5 when Roy Bailey palmed his corner into his own net. Gerry Baker scored Ipswich's consolation goal just before half time. Howfield completed his hat-trick with goals after 48 and 72 minutes while in between Bobby Robson scored another. Alan Mullery added the ninth with 2 minutes to go and, with the crowd chanting 'We want ten!', Graham Leggat curled in a shot from 30 yards over the unfortunate Bailey. Two days later Fulham lost the return match 4–2 at Portman Road.

SIXTIES LONDON CUP SUCCESS

The Cottagers' last appearance in the London Challenge Cup final came in 1966/67, when they met Brentford in the final. The first final at Griffin Park was a 0–0 draw but the Bees won the replay 2–1 at the Cottage after extra time, with Terry Dyson scoring Fulham's goal. To reach the final the Whites won at Leytonstone 5–3 and Tottenham Hotspur 4–0, and then, after a 2–2 draw at Leyton Orient, Fulham won the semi-final replay at the Cottage 5–1. Fulham's teams in the final was Ian Seymour; Dave Loveridge, Bobby Drake, Henry Hill, Brian Nichols; Hugh Cunningham, Jimmy Dunkley, Mike Pentecost; John Ryan, Terry Dyson, Terry Parmenter. Turlough O'Connor replaced Dunkley in the replayed final. The Cottagers' last game in the competition was a 1–0 home defeat against Hayes in October 1973 when it came to an end for League clubs.

FULHAM'S FIRST SUBSTITUTE

Scottish international Graham Leggat went into the club's history books as the first Fulham substitute to enter play when he came on against Chelsea in August 1965, deputising when skipper Johnny Haynes was injured. Graham said, 'It was pretty nerve-racking. You just get changed with the team, sharing the pre-match tension and while they get stuck into the game, you sit nervously watching every kick. You never know when the call is coming. When I went on after only two minutes of the second half, we were already 3–0 down. It is certainly not the best time to join in.' Leggat added, 'I felt a bit out of it at first but once I got used to the pace and warmed up it was just like any other game.' Leggat had played in the first match of the season at Blackpool but missed the next match with Blackburn Rovers with a thigh injury.

ROBSON SACKED BY FULHAM

Bobby Robson was sacked as manager of Fulham in November 1968. When interviewed about his dismissal by the *Daily Mail*, he said, 'I'm philosophical after 19 years in the game. I was promised a three-year stint then asked to go after only ten months, three of which were in the summer. The board gave me freedom to manage and made money available. I tried to sign John Toshack from Cardiff City but they wanted too much money for him. There has not been enough time for my new signings, Vic Halom and Cliff Jones, to show what they can do.' Johnny Haynes took over as caretaker-manager but lasted only four games before asking to stand down. He was replaced by his assistant Bill Dodgin who was also a former Fulham player. A 5–1 home defeat by Cardiff City was the final straw for Haynes and chairman Tommy Trinder, who was touring Australia at the time, said, 'Johnny wanted to give the players a rollicking but found it difficult if he had a poor game himself.' Haynes never wanted to be a manager and was uncomfortable from the first moment he sat behind the manager's desk, and while Robson became a very successful manager with Ipswich Town, England, PSV Eindhoven, Sporting Lisbon, Porto, Barcelona and Newcastle United, Haynes never managed again.

GEORGE COHEN TESTIMONIAL

Five of England's World Cup-winning team of 1966, plus a crowd of 18,029, paid tribute to George Cohen in a testimonial match at Craven Cottage on 10 November 1969. Skipper Bobby Moore, Gordon Banks, Geoff Hurst, Martin Peters and Nobby Stiles turned out for a World Cup XI against an International side captained by Johnny Haynes. Cohen, 30, prevented by pleurisy from playing, led out the sides. He said, 'I trained hard for this game and was going to give the fans a farewell performance to remember, but I was too ill to play after four days in bed.' Alf Ramsay, the England manager, also led the sides out. Cohen, who played 37 times for England, had his career cut short by a knee injury picked up in a match with Liverpool in December 1967. He made a brief comeback but was clearly never going to be fit enough to play top-class football again. The World Cup side beat the Internationals 10–7 and even goalkeeper Gordon Banks scored from the penalty spot.

COOK SCORES FIRST FOOTBALL LEAGUE CUP GOAL

Fulham played in the first ever League Cup tie against Bristol Rovers on 26 September 1960 and their centre forward Maurice Cook scored the first ever goal in the competition. Fulham have reached the quarter-finals on four occasions. They were in the top Division but lost at Second Division Huddersfield Town 2–1 in a replay in December 1967 but Fulham were a Third Division side by the time they lost 1–0 at Bristol City in another replay in November 1970. Just under 30 years later, on 12 January 2000, Fulham were beaten on penalties by Leicester City after a 3–3 draw, having led 3–1 at one point and the following season they lost at Liverpool 3–0 in another fifth round tie.

The largest crowd for a League Cup tie at the Cottage came in October 1970 when Fulham beat neighbours QPR 2–0 in front of 31,727. Close behind is the 29,611 who watched Fulham beat West Ham 2–1 in October 1974. The biggest crowd away from Fulham was the 30,124 that watched Spurs beat Fulham 1–0 in the fourth round in December 1981.

Fulham's biggest wins in the competition have all been in the 1960s. John Dempsey, normally a centre-half but being trialled at centre forward by manager Vic Buckingham, scored a hat-trick when they beat Northampton 5–0 at the

Cottage in October 1965. A year later Fulham beat Wolves 5–0 at home with debutant Jimmy Conway scoring with a glorious shot from 30 yards. They also defeated Workington (now a non-league side) 6–2 in October 1967 with 4 goals (a record) from Allan Clarke. Most goals scored in one tie is Fulham's 5–4 victory over Lincoln City on 21 September 2005 when Zesh Rehman, Heidar Helguson, Liam Rosenior, Tomasz Radzinski and Brian McBride scored the goals in a very entertaining match.

RECORD AWAY WIN

Fulham hit 8 goals past Halifax Town on 16 September 1969 for their record away victory. The club had just been relegated two seasons on the trot so the win signalled better times ahead. Fulham took the lead after 12 minutes when Steve Earle touched home Stan Horne's cross. Earle went on to hit a record 5 goals that evening with some lethal finishing. The other goals came from Jimmy Conway (2) and Barry Lloyd. Three other players have hit 5 goals in a league match – Fred Harrison against Stockport County in September 1908, Bedford Jezzard versus Hull City in October 1955 and Jimmy Hill at Doncaster Rovers in March 1958. Ronnie Rooke scored a double hat-trick against Bury in January 1939 in an FA Cup tie.

RECORD LEAGUE CUP CROWD

Fulham reached the quarter-finals of the League Cup for the second time despite being a Third Division club in 1970. However, they were defeated at Bristol City 1–0 after a 0–0 draw at the Cottage. To reach this point Fulham had beaten Orient, Darlington, QPR and Swindon Town. Queens Park Rangers attracted a record League Cup attendance of 31,727 to Fulham and this was the last time that over 30,000 people have attended a match at Craven Cottage. Record receipts of £9,601 were taken that evening. Rodney Marsh returned to his old stomping ground having been sold to Rangers by Fulham manager Vic Buckingham for a paltry £15,000 in March 1966, but he had a quiet game as Fulham beat their local rivals from the Second Division 2–0. Alan Morton, making his full debut for Fulham by replacing the injured Jimmy Conway, sent Steve Earle away down the left wing with a glorious 40-yard pass and Les Barrett flicked home his accurate cross to put Fulham into the lead after 14 minutes. Vic Halom deflected Barrett's shot past Rangers keeper Phil Parkes after 65 minutes to give Fulham their second goal. Ian Seymour managed to keep a clean sheet: in the Fulham goal when he pulled off an excellent save from Terry Venables' fine shot near the end of the game.

EUSEBIO OPENS RIVERSIDE

The Riverside stand was opened on 29 February 1972 with a match against Portuguese champions Benfica, who were managed by Englishman Jimmy Hagan. A good crowd of 15,606 saw a very entertaining match, which was won by the home side 3–2. Indeed, Fulham were actually 2–0 up within 20 minutes. First Steve Earle scored with a fierce shot after outstripping the Benfica defence then Earle's centre was delicately glanced into the net by Roger Cross. Jimmy Conway and Les Barrett on the wings often perplexed the Portuguese although a minute before half time Diamantio pulled a goal back for Benfica after a fine move, which had been started by Jordão. The second half was even more exciting. Coelhio sliced a shot by Cross into his own net to make the score 3–1 after 65 minutes. Three minutes later the great Eusebio scored a magnificent goal with a brilliant long-range volley. Fulham actually lost money on the night, as they had to pay their visitors £8,000 and spend another £300 to hire a generator to power the floodlights.

PELÉ COMES TO TOWN

This match was Pelé's only ever visit to London to play football and he actually scored his first and last goal in the capital in a friendly between Fulham and Santos at Craven Cottage in March 1973. He gave the 21,464 crowd a goal to remember in the 61st minute when exciting winger Edu put him away through a long pass. Suddenly Pelé burst past

John Lacy and after a 50-yard sprint, flicked the ball round goalkeeper Peter Mellor. However, just as he was about to score, Mellor grabbed his legs and brought Pelé down, so the Brazilian got up to take the penalty himself. He feinted to hit the ball to Mellor's left then smashed a wicked curler into the other side of the goal and the crowd loved it. Pelé also hit the crossbar with a 25-yard shot in the first half. Alan Pinkney, on loan from Crystal Palace, opened the scoring for Fulham from Fred Callaghan's cross after 34 minutes and Steve Earle scored the winner in the 83rd minute after a clever move. The Brazilians were supposed to attend a reception in the Benfica Bar but left the ground 30 minutes after the game. They later accused Fulham of fiddling the gate.

DEUTSCH BORE-DRAW

A friendly match with West German side MSV Duisburg ended in an extremely boring 0–0 draw before an attendance of 6,856 in Alex Stock's first home match in charge. Stock had signed Alan Mullery from Spurs for £65,000, Paul Went from Charlton Athletic for £80,000 and John Cutbush, a youngster from Tottenham's reserves, during the summer. The attack clearly lacked punch but the defence was greatly improved by these signings. Paul Went missed the game through injury but his deputy Reg Matthewson marshalled his defence well. Full-back Mike Pentecost went closest to breaking the deadlock with a sizzling shot that went just over the bar.

ANGLO-ITALIAN CUP

Fulham's first experience of European competition came in the Anglo-Italian Cup. Between February and May 1973 they played four matches against Italian opposition and drew every one. The first match was a trip to play Como and this ended 0–0. The first home game was against AS Roma, drawing 1–1 with a goal from Les Strong before a crowd of 7,712. Les Strong scored again in a 1–1 draw at Torino and the final game with Bologna was drawn 1–1 (Jimmy Conway) at Fulham.

ANGLO-SCOTTISH CUP

The Whites used the Anglo-Scottish Cup as pre-season preparation between 1975 and 1980. Fulham's best season in the competition came in 1975 when they reached the final but were defeated by Middlesbrough over two legs. Les Strong's own goal led to a 1–0 defeat at Ayresome Park and they could only draw the second leg at the Cottage 0–0. The club defeated Norwich City and Chelsea and drew with Bristol City in the preliminary round. They then beat Scottish opposition in Heart of Midlothian 5–4 on aggregate in the quarter–finals and Motherwell 4–3 on aggregate in the semi-finals. There were some good crowds with 9,672 for the home leg with Motherwell and 13,085 at the Cottage for the final with 'Boro.

BOARDROOM RUMPUS

'TRINDER QUITS IN SOCCER RUMPUS', said the headlines when he and three other directors resigned from the Fulham board as property tycoon Sir Eric Miller and Ernie Clay took control of the club. The battle, which raged for two weeks, was over £250,000 still owed to McAlpine over the building of the Riverside Stand and Miller and Clay asked for a large loan they had made to the club to be immediately repaid. The crunch came when new chairman, stockbroker Guy Libby, demanded that Miller and Clay resign. However, Libby resigned instead, as he could not raise the finance to topple Miller and Clay. When Libby resigned, Charles and Tony Dean, Derek Budden and Tommy Trinder went with him. Total debts had risen to £700,000 as Fulham had also spent heavily on the transfer market. Clay then threatened to close the club and call in the receivers and he stated that McAlpine were demanding instant payment of the debt. They denied that they had said this and stated that a family firm such as McAlpine would not close a club like Fulham down. Soon afterwards Sir Eric Miller committed suicide but Clay managed to resist another take-over by Libby, eventually making a substantial profit when he sold the club and ground to Marler Estates in 1986.

ODD END AT THE PALACE

Half the crowd of 28,733 missed the end of a promotion clash at Selhurst Park in very strange circumstances. Most were on their way home oblivious to the fact that the referee had blown up for the end of the match five minutes early because his watch had stopped. The referee, Edward Hughes from Weston-super-Mare, was convinced by his linesmen that he had seriously curtailed the half and was obliged to call the teams back out to restart the match. The third, hectic session of play lasted over five minutes. Fortunately, Fulham stopped Mr Hughes suffering further embarrassment by preventing a Palace equaliser. Fulham thoroughly deserved their 1–0 win, the winning goal coming in the 68th minute when the injured Richard Money, playing at centre forward, side-footed the ball to Brian Greenaway who advanced into the box and drove his shot hard against the inside of the post and into the net. During the third spell, Les Strong nearly scored a magnificent own goal, kicking the ball against his own post, and then Chris Guthrie scored for Fulham but it was ruled offside.

NATIONAL OPPOSITION

Fulham played England's World Cup side on 21 May 1982 as part of Les Strong's Testimonial but were soundly beaten 3–0 in front of 7,126 fans. Paul Mariner scored a couple and Bryan Robson hit the other goal. Fulham trounced England by the same score in a private friendly match in August 1961 with goals from Leggat, O'Connell and Cook.

Wales were the visitors for Gordon 'Ivor' Davies' Testimonial on 27 May 1991 and won easily 4–1 before a crowd of 3,892. The scorers for Wales were Ian Rush, Dean Saunders, David Phillips and an own goal from Jeff Eckhardt, while Robert Wilson replied for Fulham. The Welsh side included future Fulham manager Mark Hughes and future central defender Andy Melville.

ORIENTAL DELIGHT

The Japan international side was touring England and after beating a Spurs XI they visited the Cottage on 15 August 1981. The match proved a good workout for the team and Fulham narrowly won the game 2–1 before a small attendance of 1,265. A well-rehearsed free kick lead to Fulham's opener as Kevin Lock found Gordon Davies who turned and shot home, two minutes before half time. Katoh lobbed Peyton to equalise after 58 minutes but seven minutes later O'Sullivan crossed for Lewington to steer the ball home. Nobody who watched this match would have imagined that Fulham would have a Japanese player in their line-up 20 years later – Junichi Inamoto.

COLDEST NIGHT EVER

On a freezing cold night, in front of only 358 spectators, Fulham lost 3–1 to the visiting FK Austria who were making their second visit to the Cottage on 14 February 1985. The match had been postponed a couple of times before being finally played. Steinkogler scored a hat-trick for the Austrian side hitting goals after 43, 50 and 73 minutes. Ray Houghton converted Robert Wilson's cross for Fulham's consolation 9 minutes from time. FK Austria were in for preparation for a European tie with Liverpool.

RECORD LEAGUE CUP DEFEAT

Fulham's biggest defeat in domestic competitions came against Liverpool in the second round of the League Cup in September 1986. The Reds scored 10 past the unfortunate John Vaughan with goals from McMahon (4), Rush (2), Wark, Whelan and Nicol. This included 6 goals between the 63rd and 83rd minutes. Steve McMahon even managed to miss a penalty and Ian Rush hit the post twice for the Reds. Ian Rush was too sharp for the Fulham defence who failed to protect their goalkeeper. Vaughan was not the biggest goalie to play for Fulham and McMahon lobbed him for two of his four goals.

PARIS DISAPPOINTMENT

For the visit of Matra Racing of Paris on 3 August 1988, the opposition proved to be very disappointing for the meagre crowd of 1,284 who had expected to see the French side's first team but instead had to watch their reserve side that plied their trade in the French Third Division. Clive Walker scored the only goal after 35 minutes and the Whites should have scored a few more.

PROMOTION FROM THIRD DIVISION

Fulham returned to the Second Division after a memorable match with Lincoln City on 18 May 1982. If Lincoln had won they would have gone up instead of Fulham and over 20,000 people filled the Cottage in a match that had an electric atmosphere. The sending off of Steve Thompson in the 58th minute after two serious fouls helped Fulham's cause, especially as from the resulting free kick, Tony Gale lobbed the ball into the goalmouth and Roger Brown rose above everybody to head the ball home off the underside of the crossbar. Despite only having ten men, Lincoln equalised after 72 minutes through Dave Carr. The crowd suffered agony before the final whistle put them out of their misery; it was the signal for thousands of fans to flood onto the pitch and call for their heroes to make an appearance on the balcony of the Cottage. An unsung hero was Dale Tempest who replaced the injured Les Strong at left-back in the 37th minute and despite being a forward, excelled himself in that position.

HILL SAVES FULHAM FROM BRINK

The *London Standard*'s headline was, 'FULHAM SOCCER CLUB SOLD – £9M DEAL MEANS CHELSEA MAY MOVE TO SHARE CRAVEN COTTAGE'.

It was announced that the Clay family – Ernie and his sons Godfrey and Gregory, who controlled 75% of the Fulham share-holding –

are selling to S.B. Property, a subsidiary of Marler Estates, which owns Stamford Bridge, the home of Chelsea FC. S.B. Property have agreed to pay £5m cash for the entire share capital of Fulham and repay loans and creditors £3.5m. The deal means that the Clays will recover £1.6m they are owed by the club in loans and interest and take £4m of the purchase price. Fulham's new chairman will be David Bulstrode, chairman of Marler Estates, and the former chief of the Jersey Operation of Slater Walker.

The fans were glad to see the back of the Clays but the good news did not last long as the club's future would soon come into question.

'SOLD DOWN THE RIVER', exclaimed the short-lived *Daily News* headline on 24 February 1987 as it was announced that Fulham had ten weeks to live as a merger with QPR was announced for the end of the season. It was stated that the club would play under a new name at Loftus Road the following season. The Property Company called Marler Estates, which belonged to the Fulham Chairman David Bulstrode, paid Rangers' chairman Jim Gregory £5.8m for his shares. The *Daily News* stated that, 'Craven Cottage, one of the most distinctive grounds in the country, with its unique setting on the Thames, is expected to be turned into houses and flats.' Bulstrode was asked if this was the death of Fulham. He replied, 'I'm afraid it is. But it's being revived in another life.' Bulstrode was surprised by the anger this announcement produced throughout football as demonstrations and action meetings soon followed and even the Football League supported the club's survival. It was estimated that the site of Craven Cottage was worth £15m. Ironically, Gregory had supported Fulham as a boy and tried to join the board of directors in the 1960s without success – now he seemed to be playing a major role in the demise of the club. Bulstrode was surprised by the demonstrations that followed from most of the London football clubs. This included pitch protests during the game with Walsall and a meeting at Hammersmith Town Hall at which Jimmy Hill and Malcolm Macdonald talked in protest at the proposals. In March 1987 Jimmy Hill became chairman.

PUBLIC INQUIRY UNDERMINED

The headlines said, 'COUNCIL TO FIGHT HILL'S £13M PLAN'. Fulham chairman Jimmy Hill announced he had agreed a £13m deal with the club's landlords, Cabra Estates (same company as S.B.). Under the deal, Fulham would stay at their traditional home until the end of the 1990/91 season and then use the money to build a new stadium as Cabra planned to build a housing estate on the Cottage site. The fans and council were stunned by Hill's announcement and a public inquiry into the council's bid for a compulsory purchase order to buy the Craven Cottage site was started. The club received an initial £2m for a legally binding agreement to leave the Cottage, followed by £4m on vacant possession of the ground. A further £5m would be paid when Cabra received detailed planning permission followed by £2m which may be payable depending on the ultimate value of the site. This led to a pitch demonstration during the half-time period of a match with Notts County. Fans shouted 'We'll never leave the Cottage!' Hill was later subpoenaed to give evidence at the public inquiry, which the council lost without the support of the club.

SAVING CRAVEN COTTAGE

The *Daily Telegraph* ran an article on 7 October 1993 with the headline, 'GUMMER SAVES STAND IN EXTRA-TIME'. It went on to say, 'the only football stand in England which is listed as being of special architectural or historic interest, has been saved from demolition. Mr John Gummer, Environment Secretary, has dismissed two appeals over plans to redevelop Fulham's Craven Cottage ground.' The project would have involved the demolition of all but the brick façade of the Grade II listed Stevenage Road grandstand, which was built in 1905. The celebrated Craven Cottage pavilion, which is also listed, would have been converted into flats. The buildings are the earliest and one of the most unchanged, and therefore significant works, of Scotsman Archibald Leitch, who although not an architect or even a prominent engineer, was the leading football stand designer of his time. The Stevenage Road Stand is the earliest example of two-tiered design and the first in which the technique of lattice beams and trusses with curved tie members was used. The ground is also considered to be unique because of the two-storey pavilion, placed diagonally next to the stand. There used to be many of these on Scottish grounds but none have been preserved.

ASSOCIATE MEMBERS' CUP

Many supporters called this competition the 'Mickey Mouse Cup' but this was a little unfair as the final was usually played at Wembley before a sizable crowd. It has had many guises including being called the Leyland DAF Cup, the Autoglass Trophy and the Auto Windscreens Shield. Fulham first entered the competition in 1986/87, losing to Aldershot 11–10 on penalties after a 1–1 draw at the Recreation Ground. Prolific goalscorer 'Ivor' Davies managed to miss two penalties that evening and the game did not finish until after 10.30 p.m.

Fulham's only appearance at Dartford's Watling Street ground managed to attract only 937 spectators who saw the Cottagers win 6–2 against Maidstone United (they were ground sharing at the time) in October 1981. Fulham's biggest defeat in the competition came when they were comprehensively beaten 6–1 by Brighton at the Cottage in October 1987.

An oddity occurred during 1991/92 when Gillingham were the opposition on two occasions. Fulham beat them 2–0 in the preliminary round and their reward was to play them again in the following round which was also won 2–0 at Craven Cottage. Fulham's best season in the competition came in 1993/94 when they reached the Southern Area semi-final. However, they were beaten by Wycombe Wanderers 4–2 on penalties after an exciting 2–2 draw. Both Fulham goals came from Gary Brazil before a healthy crowd of 8,733.

PENALTY SHOOT-OUTS

The first shoot-out in the Football League Cup came in August 1994 when Fulham beat Luton Town 4–3 on penalties in an exciting climax to the match. The first penalty shoot-out in the FA Cup came at Brighton's Goldstone Ground on a very cold night in December 1995. After enduring a dull 0–0 draw after extra time, Fulham won the shoot-out 4–1 thanks mainly to Tony Lange. He saved a number of the penalties and also scored one himself.

PLAY-OFFS

In the early years of the century promotion issues were decided by Test matches. From the 1980s these were resurrected in the form of play-offs when clubs played each other home and away to decide promotion/relegation issues. Fulham played in their first play-off in May 1989 after finishing fourth in the old Third Division. They met Bristol Rovers in the first leg at Bath City's Twerton Park ground and lost narrowly 1–0. However, in the second leg at the Cottage, Fulham fell apart after Peter Scott was sent off for a rash challenge and eventually lost 4–0.

Fulham appeared in the play-offs again in May 1998 after finishing sixth in the Second Division. Peter Beardsley scored Fulham's goal in a 1–1 draw at the Cottage but they lost 1–0 in the return at Grimsby Town to miss out on a Wembley appearance.

QUICKEST GOALS

Rory Hamill scored Fulham's quickest ever goal in January 1995, after only 7 seconds of a match against Mansfield Town which Fulham went on to win 4–2. Hamill took advantage of a slippery surface, and a Mansfield defence that could not turn quickly on the icy pitch, to score with his first touch of the match. Earlier that season Mark Stallard scored after 14 seconds against Exeter City at the Cottage. He also scored a hat-trick in the last match of a loan spell from Derby County. Allan Jones scored after only 35 seconds of his debut against Bolton Wanderers in February 1960 but he made only a handful of appearances for Fulham before being released to join Dover.

FULHAM'S LOWEST EBB

Fulham hit rock-bottom and 91st in the Football League in January 1996 when they were defeated 2–1 at Torquay United. They faced losing their league status and relegation to the Conference after 89 years as a league club. Fulham's fans were in sombre mood after yet another defeat as the brittleness of the Londoners' defence was immediately apparent when United took the lead after only two minutes, Ian Hathaway breaking down the left and crossing for Paul Baker to turn the ball in. Mike Conroy levelled on the half-hour from close range, applying the final touch to Martin Thomas' corner. Torquay United were rewarded for their spirit, however, when Richard Hancox hooked the ball to Simon Garner to smash in the 82nd-minute winner. Manager Ian Branfoot was soon moved 'upstairs' to become General Manager and was replaced as team manager by Micky Adams who brought about a resurgence in the team which eventually rescued the club from relegation.

FULHAM ON THEIR WAY BACK

In a vital 2–1 win at Carlisle United on 5 April 1997, Rod McAree scored a wonderful goal to ensure victory before 2,000 happy travelling fans. Surprisingly recalled after six months out, McAree's goal was produced by Simon Morgan and Christer Warren, though it was his first-time shot that went in like a rocket from 20 yards. Rory Delap put the Cumbrians into the lead in the 20th minute, but Fulham hit back in the 51st minute when McAree's far post cross was headed back across goal by Danny Cullip for striker Mike Conroy to outjump two defenders on the goal line to score. After McAree's goal, Fulham goalkeeper Mark Walton made a wonderful save after 76 minutes in a one-on-one situation with Warren Aspinall. Aspinall later hit the crossbar with a shot and Nick Cusack almost scored an own goal in the dying minutes but Fulham hung on for a memorable victory. Fulham had set a new record of eleven away victories for a season. Most importantly, the win over fellow promotion-chasers Carlisle helped Fulham to runners-up spot in Division Three that season, the first success the club had had since being promoted from the old Division Three in 1981/82.

COTTAGERS TRIUMPH AT VILLA

One of the greatest moments of many during 1999 was Fulham's great FA Cup fourth round victory at top-of-the-table Aston Villa. This earned a fifth round tie at Old Trafford against Manchester United and while the headlines of the morning were all about the disappearance of Stan Collymore, the evening ones were about the Whites' great victory. Fulham took the lead after only 8 minutes when Steve Hayward swung over a beautifully weighted cross for Simon Morgan to rise and glance it past keeper Oakes. The second and clinching goal came two minutes before the break. Paul Bracewell tapped a free kick to Hayward who thumped the ball at goal. It took a deflection and looped over Oakes into the net. Paul Peschisolido, who headed against an upright, and Geoff Horsfield gave the Villa defence a torrid time and Villa never looked as though they would get back into the match. It was an especially great day for Morgan and Hayward as Morgan's family were watching the match (they were all Villa fans), and Hayward was brought up locally and had been on Villa's books as a youngster. 4,500 Fulham fans made the trip helping to form a crowd of 35,260.

INTERNATIONAL FULHAM

When Fulham beat Bury 3–1 at Loftus Road in a League Cup tie in November 2002, they fielded internationals from eleven different countries. These were: Maik Taylor (N. Ireland); Steve Finnan (Republic of Ireland), Pierre Womé (Cameroon),

Andy Melville (Wales), Abdeslam Ouaddou (Morocco); Lee Clark (England Under-21), Bjarne Goldbaek (Denmark), John Collins (Scotland); Barry Hayles (Jamaica), Junichi Inamoto (Japan), Andrejs Štolcers (Latvia), plus substitutes Facundo Sava and Martín Herrera (not capped, but from Argentina), Martin Djetou (France) and Mark Hudson (not capped).

ISRAEL UNDONE BY THE RIDDLER

An excellent crowd of 8,432 saw Fulham win comfortably 2–0 against the Israel national side at the Cottage on 3 August 1999. Simon Morgan headed home Stephen Hughes' corner to put Fulham into the lead after 22 minutes and Paul Peschisolido added a second 12 minutes after half time from close range.

Karl-Heinz Riedle scored both goals in a 2–0 victory for Fulham over the Indian national side on 23 July 2000. His first came after 40 minutes when he fired in a low shot and the second came ten minutes from time when the keeper misjudged John Collins' pass and Riedle nipped in to score.

WHAT! NO PROGRAMME?

On 17 July 2001, Fulham played Sparta Prague of the Czech Republic at Woking as the Cottage pitch was being reseeded. There is no programme for this game as Woking thought

Fulham would produce one and Fulham thought Woking would do it – or so I've been told. Therefore the 3,500 crowd had nothing to read before the game . . .

VAN DER SAR'S DEBUT

Deportivo Alavés of Spain were the visitors on 8 August 2001 for a friendly. They had been beaten by Liverpool 5–4 in the previous season's UEFA Cup final, but they won this match thanks to a goal from Navarro after 38 minutes in front of a crowd of 5,113. He deftly controlled a right wing cross and shot past new Fulham keeper Edwin van der Sar, who had been recently signed from Juventus for £7m was making his home debut. The Alavés reserve goalkeeper Martin Herrera, who Fulham later signed, spent the match sitting on the bench. van der Sar's first league game was also Fulham's first top-flight game in 33 years, as they visited Old Trafford.

TIGANA REUNION

Fulham played Monaco, one of manager Jean Tigana's former clubs, on 1 September 2001 in another friendly. After 8 minutes, John Collins centred for Zat Knight to head back across goal to set up Louis Saha to score. The second goal came after 31 minutes when Collins' free kick hit the bar and Boa Morte dived in to head home. Rool's long-range effort was deflected past Hahnemann for Monaco's goal after 56 minutes and Fulham held on for a 2–1 victory.

HOTTEST MATCH

A friendly with RCD Mallorca (Spain) was played at Loftus Road (where Fulham spent two seasons before returning to the Cottage) on what was probably the hottest day for a football match ever in the UK with temperatures at 103°F on 10 August 2003. Eto'o scored from close range to give the visitors the lead before Boa Morte headed in Volz's cross for a 31st-minute equaliser. Malbranque scored Fulham's winner after 70 minutes when he volleyed home Lee Clark's exquisite pass. The extreme heat affected the size of crowd, which was only about 1,800 and by the end of the match some of the players were struggling despite their high fitness levels.

AWAY RECORDS

A couple of records were broken during 1927/28 when, after losing their first 20 away games of the season (the club's record for away defeats in one season), Fulham won their last away game of the campaign at Notts County 1–0, thanks to a goal from Robert Ferguson. However, this did not save the club from relegation to the Third Division South.

The Cottagers' record for fewest away wins in a season is one and they achieved this in 1923/24, 1927/28, 1964/64, 1968/69, 2005/06 and 2006/07. Fulham's only away win in 2005/06 was at Manchester City and the following season their only away victory was at Newcastle United, a game in which midfield player Jimmy Bullard picked up a horrendous injury that kept him out of the game for almost 18 months.

The current record for away wins was set in 2000/01 when they won 14 games away from the Cottage with just 3 defeats, another record. This beat the previous record set in 1996/97 when 12 games were won and only 4 were lost and 1998/99 when 12 games were also won but 6 lost. This beat the previous record of 10 set in 1907/08 and 1988/89.

Fulham have terrible away records at Arsenal, Everton, Liverpool and Burnley – they've have never won a league match at the first two. Fulham have met the Gunners at three different grounds, the Manor Ground at Plumstead where they lost in the FA Cup in 1904, Highbury and the Emirates. In 24 visits, Fulham have drawn 3 and lost 21; Howfield and Haynes scored in a 2–2 draw at Highbury in 1963/64 and the Whites have drawn at Arsenal twice 0–0, in 2003/04 and 2008/09.

The Cottagers' record at Anfield is equally awful. In 24 visits, including FA and League Cup ties, they had managed just 7 draws and 17 defeats which includes a 10–0 drubbing in the League Cup. They finally won at Anfield for the first time in April 2012 thanks to an own goal. Fulham's league record at Goodison Park is also very poor and since their 0–0 at Everton in 1959/60, they have lost there 17 times on the trot and in all Fulham have lost at Everton 22 times. However, at least Fulham have won twice at Goodison in FA Cup ties in 1948 and 1974. The Cottagers' record at Turf Moor is also awful and they have not won at Burnley since 1950/51 when Bob Thomas' two goals helped the Whites to a 2–0 victory. Since then Fulham have failed to win in 27 league and cup visits. Another ground where Fulham used to have a poor record is Fratton Park where it took the club until their 12th visit before even registering a goal when Johnny Haynes scored in a 3–1 defeat in January 1969. Before this they had not scored in 4 Southern League matches and 6 Football League matches. Their first win at Portsmouth came at their 14th attempt when two goals from John Conway gave the Whites a 2–1 victory in 1972/73.

Fulham's best winning sequence away from the Cottage came in 1996/97 when they won 6 on the trot at Rochdale, Exeter City, Swansea City, Darlington, Northampton and Hull City but drew the next 0–0 at bottom club Brighton. This beat the existing record of 5 set in 1965/66 and 1981/82. Between November 1981 and January 1982, Fulham won at Carlisle United, Bristol Rovers, Swindon Town, Reading and Brentford. During the Great Escape of 1965/66, the Whites won at Leeds United, Aston Villa, West Ham United, Nottingham Forest and Northampton Town to avoid relegation.

THE CONWAY BROTHERS

Jim and John Conway, part of a family of 17, played for Fulham in the 1970s. Republic of Ireland international Jimmy Conway started his Fulham career as a wing-half but was later very effective on the right wing. He joined Fulham from Bohemians in May 1966 and during Fulham's Third Division days he was joint top scorer with 23 goals in 1969/70. Jimmy helped Fulham finish the season as runners-up in the Third Division and he also appeared at Wembley in the FA Cup final in 1975. Conway moved to Manchester City in August 1976 and he ended his career as a player with Portland Timbers in the USA where he still lives today, although he was sadly diagnosed with dementia in 2010.

John Conway also came to Fulham from the Dublin-based club Bohemians. John was unlucky with injuries at Fulham and on a number of occasions he was just beginning to establish himself in the side when he was hit by a fresh injury. He played in the first two games of Fulham's 1975 FA Cup run but lost his place and was given a free transfer just before the final.

THE LOWE BROTHERS

Eddie and Reg Lowe joined Fulham at the same time in May 1950 from Aston Villa for a joint fee of £10,000. Eddie went on to make 511 appearances for Fulham before retiring in 1963. He gained three caps for England while at Villa Park but surprisingly was never capped while at the Cottage. Eddie helped the Lilliewhites return to the First Division in 1959 and also played a major role in their FA Cup run to the semi-finals of 1962, when he appeared in every match. Eddie died in Nottingham on 9 March 2009. His brother Reg was a tall, gangling full-back who had an excellent understanding on the field with his brother before a broken leg ruined his career. His final appearance came at Luton Town in January 1953 when he broke his leg. He died in Cambridge in April 1998.

THE GOLDIE BROTHERS

Billy and Jock Goldie never played for Fulham together. Jock Goldie, a strong tackling wing–half, joined Fulham from Hurlford Thistle in May 1908, just before his brother Billy moved to Leicester Fosse in August 1908. Jock moved to Bury in September 1912 and was later banned for life from football in August 1923, three years after an incident while playing for Bury, when he and some team-mates threw a match against Coventry City which allowed them to avoid relegation. Jock died in Kingston-upon-Thames on 26 February 1958 at the age of 68. His brother Billy was a dour and gritty left-half whose aggression was feared by many of his opponents. He joined Fulham in January 1904 and rarely missed a match in his four and a half seasons at the Cottage as he helped Fulham to two Southern League titles in 1905/06 and 1906/07. Billy's strong Scottish accent was barely discernible to the Fulham management and he needed an interpreter when he went before the FA disciplinary commission. Billy later returned to his hometown of Hurlford where he died in February 1952.

THE WALLBANKS BROTHERS

Harry Wallbanks, was one of five brothers to play in the Football League – the others being Jack (Portsmouth), Fred (West Ham), Jim (Reading) and Horace (Luton). Another tough-tackling wing-half, Harry lost much of his career to the war when he worked as a miner. Nicknamed 'Choppy', he joined Fulham in October 1938 but had to wait eight years for his league debut at Bury in August 1946. Wallbanks later appeared for Southend United and Workington. He passed away in Whitehaven in April 1993.

ABANDONED MATCHES

Only seven games have been abandoned involving Fulham since joining the Football League in 1907, not counting wartime games. The referee stopped the game after 58 minutes due to a waterlogged pitch at Glossop in April 1908 with the home side a goal up. The match was replayed the following day with Fulham finding victory 2–1 with the help of an own goal and a finish from Bob Carter. The Lilliewhites had two games abandoned in an eight-day spell during December 1946. The first was against Nottingham Forest at the Cottage on the 14th and the second came a week later at Southampton. The Forest game was abandoned due to fog after 70 minutes and the game at the Dell because of frost after 78 minutes with wing-half Pat Beasley scoring in a 1–1 draw.

An FA Cup tie with Grimsby Town at the Cottage ended at the interval in January 1954 with the Whites winning the replayed match 3–1. A Third Division encounter at Rochdale in November 1969 was called off after 69 minutes owing to an icy pitch, much to the disappointment of the 6,391 crowd. A Jim Conway penalty and a 25-yard shot from Johnny Haynes for Fulham were cancelled out with goals from Tony Buck and Hugh Riley for Rochdale. The last time we were involved with an abandoned game was at Roker Park on

8 April 2006 against Sunderland. Fulham were winning 1–0 thanks to a goal from Brian McBride when the match was abandoned after 21 minutes after a torrential downpour and sleet and snow made the pitch unplayable. The Whites lost the replayed match.

CHAIRMEN

There have been eleven chairmen since the club became a Limited Company in 1903. The longest-serving chairman was John Dean who served from 1903 to 1907 and then from 1925 to 1944. He initially resigned in 1907 when he had a disagreement with director Henry Norris who took over as chairman. Norris was replaced a year later by William Hall but when they both departed to Arsenal in 1913 they were replaced by William Allen. James Watt took over in 1924 but the following year John Dean returned to the helm. When Dean died in 1944 his son Charles took over at the top. The famous comedian Tommy Trinder replaced Charles Dean in 1958 and he was chairman until 1977 when Guy Libby took over briefly. Ernie Clay won a boardroom battle and became chairman before the start of 1977/78. His period in charge was ultimately a disaster as he ran the club down by selling off their best players before selling out to Marler Estates in 1986. David Bulstrode became chairman until he announced the merger of the club with QPR and Jimmy Hill and Bill Muddyman put together a new consortium to take over the club in April 1987. Current chairman Mohammed Al Fayed replaced them in April 1997.

CHAMPIONS

The Cottagers have only finished the season as champions of their respective division on six occasions since becoming a Limited Company in 1903. Fulham were champions of the Southern League First Division in 1905/06 where they conceded just 15 goals (and only conceded more than one goal in a match on one occasion at the Dell) and were defeated in only three games all season. Manager Harry Bradshaw took Fulham to their second successive Southern League title the following season thus carrying out his promise to take the club into the Football League. Fulham conceded only 32 goals during the entire season and were defeated only once at home. Fulham's half-back line of Pat Collins, Billy Morrison and Billy Goldie were outstanding as was goalkeeper Jack Fryer over this two-season period.

Fulham won the Third Division South championship in 1931/32 with 57 points, two ahead of runners up Reading. Striker 'Bonzo' Newton, Fulham's bustling centre forward, scored a record 43 goals out of a record 111 during the season, 72 of these coming in matches at the Cottage. Despite being a Third Division side, Fulham's half-back line included two England internationals in Albert Barrett and Len Oliver.

The Lilliewhites clinched the Second Division title on the last day of the 1948/49 season with a 2–0 win over West Ham. Southampton should have won the title but threw their chance away with a run of poor results at the end of the campaign. Fulham were promoted with West Bromwich Albion and the Saints manager Bill Dodgin left the Dell to manage the Whites in their first top-flight season. Bob Thomas was Fulham's leading goalscorer with 23 followed closely behind by Arthur Rowley who hit 19 goals in only 22 appearances after signing from West Brom in December 1948.

Fulham ran away with the Second Division championship in 1998/99. The title was sewn up in April and by the end of the season the club had passed the 100 points mark. They had won 31 games, lost only seven and scored 79 goals and conceded just 32. It all ended on a sour note when manager Kevin Keegan was enticed away to become the new England manager.

Fulham won their first 11 games of 2000/01 under the management of Frenchman Jean Tigana. In a record-breaking season, the Whites ran away with title to gain a return to the top flight for the first time in 33 years. Tigana's best buy was the £2m he paid Metz for striker Louis Saha who went on to score 32 goals in just 27 appearances in the league that season. Barry Hayles and Luis Boa Morte also hit another 40 goals between them.

CRAVEN COTTAGE

Fulham purchased the grounds of Craven Cottage in 1894 but it took two years to develop the site into a football ground. The original Craven Cottage was built in 1780 but had burned down in 1888 and the area became derelict. It was one of the many properties close to the Thames which wealthy people used as their retreats away from the grime of London. The first match at the revamped Cottage was a Middlesex Senior Cup tie against Minerva on 10 October 1896, which Fulham won easily by 4–0. The terraces at this time were mud banks made up from the material excavated from the Shepherd's Bush to Bank tube line which was being built at the time. A large wooden stand, which became known as the 'Rabbit Hutch', was built in about 1903 but was soon condemned as unsafe and the ground was completely rebuilt in 1905.

The present Stevenage Road stand and the Cottage were designed and built by the ground designer Archibald Leitch, and the mud banks were properly terraced with stone. The ground remained unchanged until 1959 when extensions to the terraces were built at the Putney and Hammersmith Ends. Floodlights came, after a long wait, in 1962 and the Hammersmith End was roofed in 1965 with money from Alan Mullery's transfer to Tottenham Hotspur. After the terrible fire in May 1985 at Valley Parade (Bradford City's ground) in which over 50 people perished, the Stevenage Road stand was closed for remedial work for half a season. The Riverside Stand was built in 1972 but by the early 1990s was looking a sad sight and clearly in need of refurbishment which took place in 1997.

The club were seeking to completely rebuild the Cottage after their return to the top flight in 2001 and although they were allowed to use standing areas during their first season in the Premier League, the club decided to ground share at Loftus Road in 2002 while the ground was completely rebuilt. After two seasons sharing with Queens Park Rangers, and after much campaigning by the fans, the Thamesiders returned to a refurbished Craven Cottage for the start of the 2004/05 season. The improvements had been scaled down but the Putney and Hammersmith Ends were converted to seating areas as was the Stevenage Road stand which was later renamed the Johnny Haynes stand in memory of the maestro who passed away in 2005.

EDUCATED PLAYERS

As well as Skene, Berry and Hegazi who have already been mentioned, Scottish International centre forward Bobby Hamilton was a man of considerable accomplishments both on and off the pitch. Bobby Hamilton's calculating methods were not at first appreciated by the Fulham crowd but the Scottish forward possessed exquisite style and was famous for his lethal long-range shooting. Bobby gained honours galore with Rangers, including four league championship medals and three Scottish Cup medals. After spending a season at Fulham, in which they won the Southern League title, Hamilton decided to return to Rangers in May 1907. He had a Master of Arts degree from Glasgow University and was later a very successful businessman and ran his family's net-making business. He eventually became the Lord Provost of his hometown Elgin and was also the chairman of Moray & Nairn Education Committee from 1934 until 1937.

Recent brainy Fulham footballers include: Julian Hails who had a BA (Hons) in Maths from Surrey University and is currently head of Mathematics at a school in Hertfordshire. John Lacy, who played at centre-half in Fulham's FA Cup final side of 1975, was a graduate from the London School of Economics and Jim Hicks, a centre-half from the mid-1980s, had attended Warwick University and St Luke's College, Exeter, before coming to the Cottage. Three players from

Fulham's promotion side of 1996/97 also had degrees. These were Nick Cusack, Matt Lawrence (American Literature) and Mark Blake (Business Studies).

Another player with a degree from London University, and who played just once for the Whites, was Maurice Edelston. Egyptian Hussein Hegazi also attended both Cambridge and London Universities but dropped out twice. A winger from the 1930s, Howard Fabian, went to Cambridge and later became a master at Highgate School.

ENGLAND INTERNATIONALS

Eleven Fulham players have appeared for England while with the Whites. These are John Arnold, Bert Barrett, George Cohen, Johnny Haynes, Bedford Jezzard, Jim Langley, Len Oliver, Frank Osborne, Jim Taylor and most recently Zat Knight and Bobby Zamora. Fulham's first England International was Frank Osborne who appeared in a 2–0 win over Ireland at The Hawthorns in October 1922. The Cottagers' most capped player is Johnny Haynes with 56 caps, followed by George Cohen with 37. Paul Parker played in the World Cup semi-final in 1990 (three years after leaving Craven Cottage) and, of course, George Cohen and Bobby Moore helped England to their 1966 World Cup success at Wembley. Former Fulham players Ron Greenwood and Bobby Robson have managed their country and Kevin Keegan left his post as Fulham's manager to take over the national side. Recent England Internationals to also appear for Fulham are Peter Beardsley, Paul Bracewell, Andy Cole, Stan Collymore,

John Salako and Brian Talbot. In recent years Jimmy Bullard, Sean Davis and David Stockdale were selected for England squad but have not yet appeared for their country, although Bobby Zamora made his England debut in 2010.

RECORD FA CUP VICTORY

One of the few highlights of 1995 was a record FA Cup 7–0 victory over Swansea City in November. Mike Conroy opened the scoring after only 3 minutes and he also added the second 15 minutes later when Martin Thomas' shot was half saved by keeper Freestone allowing Conroy to walk the ball in. After 18 minutes Paul Brooker replaced the injured Lea Barkus and went on to have an outstanding match. Duncan Jupp scored the third from Brazil's corner in the 28th minute and Conroy scored from close range to complete his hat-trick. Terry Angus' forceful header allowed Nick Cusack to add the fifth and Paul Brooker scored a deserved goal for the sixth from Danny Bolt's deep cross. Martin Thomas added Fulham's seventh for the record, with a left-foot volley, ten minutes from the end.

Fulham first entered the FA Cup in 1896 and lost to Swanscombe in Kent 5–0 in their first tie. Fulham's biggest FA Cup defeat came at Queens Park Rangers in November 1901 when they lost 7–0 in a third qualifying round tie. Fulham also hold the record for the biggest defeat in a semi-final when we lost to Newcastle United 6–0 at Anfield in March 1908. Keeper Les Skene's injury did not help as the defence struggled to hold back the stream of Newcastle attacks.

The Cottagers also hold the record for the number of games played before reaching the final. They played 11 games on their way to the final in 1975, playing Hull City three times and Nottingham Forest on four occasions before winning through. The Forest tie seemed to go on and on – after three drawn ties, two at the Cottage and one at the City Ground, two goals from Viv Busby finally brought the Whites a 2–1 victory. First Division leaders Everton were beaten 2–1 at Goodson Park in the fifth round and Les Barrett hit the winner at Carlisle United in the quarter-final to set up a semi-final tie with Birmingham City. John Mitchell's last-gasp winner in the replay over Birmingham City at Maine Road, Manchester, secured Fulham's first and only visit to Wembley. Unfortunately they lost 2–0 to West Ham in the final to two Alan Taylor goals. Future Fulham manager Bobby Campbell later tried to sign Taylor to boost the Fulham attack.

Fulham had reached four semi-finals – in 1908, 1936, 1958 and 1962 – before finally succeeding in reaching the final in 1975. They also reached the semi-final in 2002 but lost 1–0 to Chelsea at Villa Park. They have also lost at the quarter-final stage on 8 occasions – in 1905, 1912, 1926, 1948, 1951, 2004, 2009 and 2010. On the down side, Fulham have lost twice to non-league opposition (not including pre-1920 Southern League clubs) when they were defeated at the Cottage by Hayes 2–0 on 15 November 1991 and exactly two years later lost at Yeovil Town 1–0 in a televised match.

FATHER AND SON

There have been three father and son combinations at Fulham. The first was the Bradshaws in the first decade of the twentieth century. Harry was the manager of Fulham from April 1904 until May 1909 and two of his sons, William and Joseph, joined Fulham from Woolwich Arsenal where their father had also been the boss. Joe played only nine games for the first team in five seasons but later managed the club from May 1926 until May 1929. Will played only five times for Fulham, scoring two goals.

Joe and Maurice Edelston both played for Fulham. Joe joined Fulham from Manchester City in November 1920 and by the time Maurice arrived at Fulham in July 1935, his father was assistant manager. When manager Jack Peart sacked Joe in 1937, father and son moved to Brentford. Maurice went on to become a prolific goalscorer for Reading.

The final father and son pairing are the Dodgins; Bill (Senior) managed Fulham from September 1949 until December 1952 and his son Bill (Junior) played for Fulham around the same time although he was forced to move to Arsenal when the boo-boys started giving him stick because of his father's lack of success. When Fulham lost 2–1 to Bristol Rovers in the FA Cup in November 1970, Bill (Junior) was in charge at Fulham and Bill (Senior) managed Rovers.

FOOTBALL COMBINATION

This competition started life in 1915 as the London Combination, a regional wartime competition for clubs in the London area. After the war ended, it became a reserve league for Southern clubs including Fulham. Fulham finished as champions of the 'A' section in 1949/50 but lost the championship decider to 'B' section champions Charlton Athletic 5–1. Fulham also finished as runners-up in 1932/33 (when they were runners-up to Brentford by just one point and scored 112 goals) and 1968/69. The second occasion that Fulham finished as runners-up was extraordinary as the first team was relegated to the Third Division in 1968/69. The reserves often had an international forward line including Johnny Haynes, Johnny Byrne, Cliff Jones and future star Malcolm Macdonald and they finished four points behind champions Arsenal. The club finally won the Combination in 1998/99.

FOOTBALL LEAGUE & PREMIERSHIP CHAMPIONS

The first Fulham-connected player to collect a league championship medal was tough Scottish defender Billy Goldie with Liverpool in 1898/99 followed closely by England international wing-half Albert Wilkes with Aston Villa the following season. Luis Boa Morte, Stephen Hughes (both fringe players with Arsenal in 1998) and Andy Cole have all won the Premiership. Cole, who played for Fulham in two separate periods, has actually won four Premiership medals for Manchester United from 1995 to 2000. Six players have won two medals: Paul Parker (Manchester United) in 1993 and 1994, Pat Beasley (Arsenal) 1934 and 1935, George Best (Manchester United) 1965 and 1967, Ray Houghton and Peter Beardsley (Liverpool) 1988 and 1990, and Jack Lambert (Arsenal) 1931 and 1933. Roy Bentley and Ron Greenwood were players under manager Ted Drake when Chelsea won the title in 1955. In recent years Edwin van der Sar has won four Premier League Champions medals with Manchester United and Louis Saha and Chris Smalling have each won one. Damien Duff, Wayne Bridge and Eidur Gudjohnsen have also won them with Chelsea.

FOOTBALL LEAGUE CUP FINALS

22 Fulham players have played in the League Cup final with other clubs. Three players have won two medals: Paul Parker (Manchester United – a winners' medal in 1992 but a losers' two years later), Ray Houghton who scored in Oxford United's 3–0 victory over QPR in 1986 and was a non-playing substitute for Aston Villa in 1994, and finally Peter Storey played in two losing finals for Arsenal in 1968 and 1969 when they lost to Third Division Swindon Town. They were not the first team from the Division Three to win the trophy – QPR achieved this in the first League Cup final at Wembley in 1967 and former Fulham players Jim Langley and Rodney Marsh appeared in Rangers' line up.

In recent years, Fulham-connected players Mark Schwarzer, Damien Duff, Eidur Gudjohnsen, Edwin van der Sar, Steve Finnan, Steed Malbranque, Geoff Horsfield, Andy Cole, Danny Murphy and Wayne Bridge have all appeared in League Cup finals.

FOOTBALL LEAGUE REPRESENTATIVES

Representing the Football League used to be almost as a high an honour as winning a cap for your country. The games were mainly against the Scottish League, the Italian League, the Irish League and League of Ireland sides. These matches gradually died out and virtually disappeared after the 1960s. Johnny Haynes has played the most times for the Football League – 14 times. Bobby Moore, who later played for Fulham, appeared 12 times while with the Hammers. The Football League side was usually made up of English players but Welsh wing wizard Cliff Jones played three times while at Tottenham Hotspur: Cliff joined Fulham from Spurs in 1968 but was past his best by this time.

GREATEST GOALSCORERS

Gordon Davies heads the list of all-time Fulham goalscorers with 180 goals. These are made up of 159 league, 8 FA Cup, 11 League Cup and 2 others. Below Ivor are: Johnny Haynes 158, Bedford Jezzard 155, Jim Hammond 151, Graham

Leggat 134, Arthur Stevens 124, Steve Earle 109, Maurice Cook 97, Les Barrett 92 and Frank Newton 81. Earle and Barrett's totals include other games such as the Watney Cup and Anglo-Scottish and Anglo-Italian Cups. In league matches only, Gordon Davies again tops the list with 159 goals followed by Jezzard 155, Haynes 147, Hammond 142, Leggat 127, Stevens 110, Earle 98, Cook 89, Newton 77, Robson 77.

HANDBOOKS & BROCHURES

Fulham first produced a handbook for the 1904/05 season and this included fixtures and tables, an early history of the club and pen pictures and photographs of all the players and staff. The handbook was produced until 1913/14 and provided a great source of photographs and information on players who appeared for the club at that time. It is not clear whether handbooks were produced regularly in the inter-war period. However, there was a handbook for 1934/35, which, again, had some excellent photos of the players. The 1948/49 handbook included an article written by Dudley Evans who was a director of the club. This was called 'The Old Brigade' and was about some of the players who had appeared for Fulham over the years. The following season's handbook contained a photograph of the Fulham side that toured the West Country over Easter 1892.

The supporters' club produced a handbook from 1954/55 to 1961/62, which was similar to those that had gone before except they used action photos and team groups for the first time. The club again produced handbooks from 1966/67 to 1972/73, the last season appearing as part of the club's official programme. There were also special publications to celebrate promotions. The first of these was in 1982 followed by a promotion review called *Fulham's Going Up* in 1997 and champions in 1998/99 and 2000/01. The club also published handbooks covering seasons 2002/03 to 2005/06.

HOME RECORDS

A new record for home wins of 19 in a season was created in 1998/99 when Fulham won the Second Division title. The only defeat of the season was at home to Luton Town in October. The previous record of 18 wins was set in 1958/59 when only 21 home games were played and 18 were won, 1 drawn and 2 lost. The only games in which Fulham were not victorious were against Liverpool (1–0) and Swansea Town (2–1) and a draw with Scunthorpe United.

The fewest home wins in a season came in 1951/52 with only 5 when the Cottagers were relegated from the First Division. Fulham suffered a record 11 defeats in 1967/68 and 1979/80, both relegation seasons, and in the latter Fulham scored their fewest goals in a season with a paltry 19 in 21 games. The biggest win of the season was 3–1 over Burnley and they managed to score no more than one goal on three other occasions.

Fulham hit home a record 72 goals during 1931/32 when they finished as Third Division South champions. This included three 5-goal bonanzas plus 8 against Thames and 10 against Torquay United.

Goalkeeper Arthur Reynolds and the Fulham defence conceded only 8 goals in 21 home matches during 1921/22 but this was before the change in the offside law in 1926 which led to more goals being scored.

Southampton have not won in the league or cup at Craven Cottage since 1947/48 (13 visits). Bradford City have not won in the league since 1936/37 but beat Fulham in the League Cup in 1987/88. Walsall (10 games) and Darlington (8) have never won at Fulham and Rochdale have never, ever beaten Fulham in 11 matches home or away.

INTERNATIONALS AT FULHAM

Fulham had the great honour of the England international side playing at Craven Cottage when Wales were the visitors on 18 March 1907 for a Home International fixture. A crowd of over 20,000 attended the match and Wales were the better side in the first half. The mercurial Billy Meredith created some chances and entertained the crowd with his marvellous skill – he was one of the great players of his era. Meredith's run and centre paved the way for Billy 'Lot' Jones to put the Welsh ahead. England were disappointing as players like Wall and Stewart failed to recreate their club form, but the star of the England side was the great Steve Bloomer who helped England put on a great deal of pressure in the second half. Stewart finally equalised for England to earn a 1–1 draw despite Leigh Richmond Roose having an excellent match in goal for Wales in the second half.

The second international was between Northern Ireland and Cyprus in May 1973. The match was played in London due to the troubles in Ulster. This was a World Cup qualifying match that was won by the Irish 3–0 with goals from Trevor Anderson (two) and another from Sam Morgan before an attendance of 7,000. George Best did not appear for the Irish.

Australia have played four Internationals at Craven Cottage in recent years: 16 November 2004 v Norway, 9 June 2005 v New Zealand, 9 October 2005 v Jamaica and 17 November 2007 v Nigeria. Other internationals have been played on 26 March 2008 between Ghana and Mexico, 18 November 2009 between Serbia and North Korea and on 5 September 2011 when Brazil and Ghana were the opponents. On top of this England played Argentina in an under-21 International on 27 February 2000, the English side featuring Fulham's Sean Davis.

LEAGUE OF IRELAND

Jimmy Conway and Turlough O'Connor, who arrived at Fulham from Bohemians (Dublin) in May 1966, both represented the League of Ireland. Conway was only 17 when he played for the League against the Irish League in May 1965, and O'Connor appeared on three occasions. The first was in March 1973 when the League of Ireland lost 2–0 to the Italian League. A year later they beat the Irish League 3–2 and in October 1984 they lost 4–0 to the Irish League with O'Connor in the side. Additionally, Alan Gough played for the League of Ireland against Manchester United in August 1996. John Conway won a League of Ireland Cup winners' medal when he helped Bohemians beat Sligo Rovers

2–1 after two replays in 1970 and Turlough O'Connor also won a winners medal when Bohemians beat Drogheda in April 1976. Sean Maher, who played a couple of games for Fulham in 1997/98, helped Bohemians to a league and cup double in 2000/01 before returning to league football with Bournemouth.

MANAGERS

The first manager to be appointed by Fulham came in April 1904. This was Harry Bradshaw who took Fulham to two Southern League titles and into the Football League. Statistically he is the Cottagers' most successful manager. The least successful was Bobby Robson whose teams won only 6 of their 36 matches whilst he was in charge of the club. The longest-serving managers are Phil Kelso from May 1909 until May 1924 (15 years) and Jack Peart from May 1935 until September 1948 (13 years). The shortest-serving is Ray Wilkins (September 1997 to May 1998) and Lawrie Sanchez (April to December 2007) who were in charge for only 8 months. Ray Lewington was Fulham's youngest manager being just 29 years and 10 months old when he took over as player-manager in July 1986. Bedford Jezzard, who had been forced to retire due to injury in 1957 was 10 months older than Lewington when he became the manager in June 1958.

Roy Hodgson is Fulham's oldest serving manager. He was born at West Croydon on 9 August 1947 and resigned as manager of Fulham in July 2010 to take over at Liverpool at the age of 62 years and 11 months. Dugald Livingstone had previously been Fulham's oldest manager at 60 years and 3 months (b. Alexandria, Dumbartonshire, 25 February 1898) when he resigned in May 1958.

MERGERS

There have been two attempts to merge the club. Former chairman Henry Norris, who was chairman of Woolwich Arsenal, attempted to merge Arsenal and Fulham and his plan was for the newly merged club to play at White City. This would have been a catastrophe as two attempts by QPR to play there ended in failure in 1932 and 1963 because the stadium lacked atmosphere and the crowds were very disappointing. Norris eventually gave up on the plan and moved Arsenal from Plumstead to Highbury in September 1913.

The second attempt at a merger came in February 1987 when Fulham chairman David Bulstrode announced that he was going to close down Fulham and merge the club with Queens Park Rangers. This led to mass demonstrations at many of the London clubs and included half-time pitch invasions at the Cottage. Bulstrode had taken on more than he had anticipated and in the end sold the club to Jimmy Hill's new consortium in April 1987 and the club survived.

FA AMATEUR CUP

Until 1974 the major competition in non-league circles was the FA Amateur Cup, the final of which was played at Wembley after 1948. Many players have appeared in these finals before they became professional at Fulham. The first such player was Alf Harwood, who played and scored for Crook Town in 1901 when they beat King's Lynn 3–0. The following year he appeared for Bishop Auckland who lost 5–1 to Old Malvernians. The Farnfield brothers, Herbert and Percy, appeared for Clapton in the 1905 final where they lost to West Hartlepool 3–2 at Shepherd's Bush (Loftus Road) and Arthur Berry played for South Bank in 1913 when they lost to Oxford City in the final.

After the First World War, Alf Pilkington helped Dulwich Hamlet beat Tufnell Park 1–0 at the Den before 25,000 and in the next two seasons Sid Binks played in two victorious finals for Bishop Auckland. He scored twice in both finals, a 4–2 victory over Swindon Victoria in 1920 and a 5–2 victory over South Bank the following year.

Another future Fulham player, Jim McCree, appeared in the 1923 final for London Caledonians and he scored in their 2–1 victory. Fred Avey helped Leyton beat Durham village side Cockfield 3–2 in 1928 and Bill Caesar was on the losing side when Hayes lost to Wycombe Wanderers in 1931. Other Fulham-connected players to win medals before the Second World War were Bill Dowden with Wimbledon in 1935 and Bernard Joy and Howard Fabian the following year with the Casuals.

Three players have appeared in the FA Amateur Cup final since the war. Reg Stratton helped Woking beat Ilford 3–0 in

1958 before a crowd of 71,000 at Wembley, but Alan Mansley had the heartbreak of seeing his colleague Alan Bermingham miss a penalty in the last minute of extra time to draw 0–0 with Enfield, before losing the replay 3–0. Finally, Richard Teale appeared in the penultimate final for Walton & Hersham when they beat Slough Town 1–0 in 1973. Former Fulham goalkeeper Doug Flack managed the Corinthian Casuals side that lost to Bishop Auckland 4–1 in the 1956 final replay.

FA TROPHY

Seven players with a first team connection to Fulham have appeared in the FA Trophy final at Wembley. These are Laurence Batty (1994, 1995 and 1997), Brian Cottington (1988), Brian Greenaway (1985), Jack McClelland (1972), Simon Stewart (1999 and 2000), Mark Tucker (1994 and 1995), and Clive Walker (1994, 1995, 1997 and 1998). Batty, Tucker and Walker appeared together in the 1994 and 1995 finals when Woking beat Runcorn 2–1 and Kidderminster Harriers 2–1. Walker has played in four finals and has been on the winning side in each. He played for Woking again in the 1997 final when they beat Dagenham & Redbridge 1–0 and the following season with Cheltenham Town who beat Southport 1–0.

Jack McClelland appeared between the sticks in Barnet's 3–0 defeat against Stafford Rangers in 1972. Brian Greenaway helped Wealdstone to the Trophy and Conference double in 1985 and Brian Cottington joined Enfield just before the reached the final and beat Telford United 3–2 in a replay.

Simon Stewart has appeared in the two finals for Kingstonian and in recent years, John Hamsher played in the 2002 final for Stevenage Borough at Villa Park but was on the losing side to Yeovil 2–0.

FA VASE

Brian O'Connell and Trevor Lee played for Epsom & Ewell in the first FA Vase final in 1975, Andy Thomas was player-manager for Oxford City in 1995 and Martin Pike appeared for Bedlington Terriers in 1999. They all finished on the losing side. Mark Blake appeared in the 2004 final for Winchester City against AFC Sudbury but his team lost 2–0.

OLDEST PLAYER

The oldest player to appear for Fulham is Wattie White who was 40 years and 275 days old when he played for the club at Bury on 14 February 1923. He was born in Hurlford, Ayrshire, on 15 May 1882. The man in second place is Wilf Nixon who lived until 102 – he was 39 years and 190 days old when he played his final match in goal on 30 April 1921. Nixon was born at Gateshead on 2 October 1882.

Trainer Jimmy Sharp was called out of retirement on 30 April 1921 and played in an emergency when forward Harold Crockford missed the coach to the game. Sharp even scored a rare goal in his last ever game.

The top ten oldest players are as follows:

Wattie White	40 years 275 days
Wilf Nixon	39 years 190 days
Jimmy Sharp	39 years 189 days
Joe Bacuzzi	39 years 83 days
Jimmy Croal	38 years 245 days
Glenn Cockerill	38 years 40 days
Andy Ducat	38 years 27 days
Kevin Moore	38 years 7 days
Frank Penn	37 years 350 days
Arthur Stevens	37 years 278 days

YOUNGEST PLAYER

The youngest player to make his first team debut for Fulham is Matt Briggs who was 16 years and 65 days old when he played against Middlesbrough on 13 May 2007. Paul Parker and Jeff Hopkins were both 17 years and 21 days old when they made their Fulham debuts. Sean Davis is fourth on the list as he was 17 years and 25 days old when he came on as substitute against Cambridge United in October 1996 and Tony Mahoney is the fifth youngest, being 17 years and 38 days old on his Fulham debut.

OPPOSITION RECORDS

Which team has gone the longest since winning at Craven Cottage? Darlington (8), Halifax Town (3), Hereford United (5), Rochdale (5) and Walsall (14) have never won in the league or cup at Fulham (the number of visits is in brackets). Walsall did, however, beat Fulham 5–2 at Craven Cottage in the Auto Windscreens Cup in 1995. Bradford City last won a league encounter at Fulham in 1936/37 when they won 1–0, but the Bantams did win 5–1 at Fulham in a League Cup match September 1987. Newport County last won at the Cottage in 1930/31 but have visited only on five occasions since and have now left the league. Coventry City last won at the Cottage in 1947/48 but they have only visited three times since and Southampton have not won at our Stevenage Road ground since 1947/48 when they won 2–0. Since this victory the Saints have played eight league and two cup games at Fulham without success.

PENALTIES

There are no accurate records of who are the most successful penalty-takers in Fulham's history but the most successful since the war have been Jim Langley and Kevin Lock. Langley scored 33 goals for Fulham between 1957 and 1965 and 19 of these were from the penalty spot. He rarely missed for Fulham but missed one at Wembley while playing for England. Kevin Lock scored 29 goals for the Whites between 1978 and 1985 and 22 of these were penalties. Charlie Mitten once scored a hat-trick of penalties for Manchester

United before his arrival at the Cottage, this coming in March 1950 against Aston Villa. Cliff Carr missed two in a game against Shrewsbury Town in February 1984. Fortunately for him, Fulham still won 3–0 with goals from Coney, Rosenior and Davies. Five players have scored two penalties in the same game for Fulham – Fred Maven, Jimmy Torrance, Jack Papworth, Syd Gibbons and Arthur Stevens.

RELEGATION

Fulham have been relegated on six occasions since joining the Football League in 1907. The worst of these was when the club dropped from the First to the Third Division between 1967 and 1969. Over this two-season period, Fulham gained only 52 points out of a possible 168 (2 points for a win). In 1967/68 they conceded 98 goals and won just 10 games out of 42. The following season Fulham won only 7 games all season.

Fulham's first relegation came in 1927/28 when they obtained only 2 points from a possible 42 in away matches and dropped into the Third Division for the first time. The Whites' worst spell was when they were relegated into the Third Division in 1994. With the club at its lowest ebb, Fulham needed to beat Swansea City in the last game but lost 2–1 while Blackpool beat Leyton Orient 4–1 to survive. Fulham were also relegated from the First to the Second Division in 1951/52 when they finished bottom with only 27 points, and in 1979/80 when we were relegated to the Third Division and scored only 19 goals in our 21 home games.

SCOTTISH INTERNATIONALS

21 players who have appeared for Fulham have been capped by Scotland, but only two while playing for the club, these being Jimmy Sharp and Graham Leggat. Sharp made his last appearance for the Scots while a Fulham player in March 1909 when they lost to Wales 3–2 at Wrexham. Leggat was capped 18 times for Scotland, 11 while at Fulham, in which he scored 6 goals. His last international appearance came in June 1960 in a 3–3 draw in Hungary.

John Collins is the most capped Fulham-connected Scottish player with 58 caps. Steve Archibald, who played 2 games for Fulham in the early 1990s, was capped 27 times, Leggat 18, Alex Forbes 14 and Bobby Templeton and Bobby Hamilton follow him with 11 each. Forbes played a handful of matches for Fulham in the 1950s while Hamilton won a Southern League champions medal in his only season at Fulham in 1906/07.

Bobby Templeton was one of the most famous players in the early years of the twentieth century, appearing for Fulham from 1913 to 1915. A brilliant dribbler with superb ball control and tactical genius, Bobby was a great favourite with the crowds as he was a great entertainer. He could sometimes drive his colleagues wild with anger, however, as he was often seen to show off his ball skills rather than pass to another player. He was a genuine Edwardian dandy, immaculately dressed and popular with women, and he once won a gold medal for getting into a cage with a lion and twisting its tail. He gained 11 caps for Scotland, making his debut against England in May 1902, scoring a goal in a 2–2 draw. One of his body swerves was said to have caused the Ibrox disaster of that year when the crowd lost its balance watching him. Templeton stayed at Fulham for two seasons but had lost some of his zip by this time and returned to Kilmarnock in April 1915, retiring soon afterwards. He was a publican in Kilmarnock when he died of heart failure after a bout of influenza in November 1919, at the early age of 40.

SCOTTISH LEAGUE CHAMPIONS

Ten Fulham players have won Scottish league championship medals. The first was Bobby Hamilton who won four on the trot with Glasgow Rangers from 1899 to 1902. Archie Gray, who played for Fulham just before the First World War, won his with Hibernian in 1902/03 before moving south to join Woolwich Arsenal, while Bobby Graham and Willie Wardrope helped Third Lanark to their only league title in 1903/04 and they both moved to Fulham the following season. Bobby Templeton helped Glasgow Celtic to the double in 1906/07 and he appeared for Fulham from 1913 to 1915. The Scot Archie Macaulay, who played for Fulham from 1950, helped Glasgow Rangers win the Scottish title in 1934/35 before moving south to join West Ham United. More recent winners have been Graham Leggat at Aberdeen in 1954/55, Steve Archibald and Doug Rougvie at Aberdeen in 1979/80 and Rougvie did it again in 1983/84 under the expert management of Alex Ferguson. Most recently, former Fulham midfielder Terry Hurlock won a Scottish league medal with Rangers in 1990/91, Bobby Petta helped Celtic to the title in 2000/01 and Steve Davis has picked up three

Scottish league titles, plus Scottish League Cup and FA Cup medals with Rangers.

SCOTTISH LEAGUE REPRESENTATIVES

Although now no longer fashionable, league representative sides used to be nearly as important as international sides, especially in the days when few internationals were played. The Scottish League side was made up entirely of players plying their trade in the Scottish League and eleven players who later moved to the Cottage have played for the Scottish League. Near the turn of the century Jimmy Sharp, Les Skene, Bobby Templeton, Willie Wardrope, Jimmy Croal, Archie Gray, Bobby Hamilton and William Lennie all represented the Scottish League. Since the Second World War Peter Marinello, Des Bremner and Graham Leggat have also done so. Hamilton played 7 times for the Scottish League and Leggat 5 times.

SEMI-PROFESSIONAL INTERNATIONALS

Semi-professional internationals are a recent phenomena, having only started in the late 1980s. Barry Hayles was capped twice during his time with Stevenage Borough and Kevin Betsy won a cap at Woking. The other caps are Laurence Batty (Woking) with 4, Corey Browne (Dover Athletic) with 3, David Harlow (Farnborough) with 2,

Mark Newson (Maidstone United) with 6 and Mark Tucker (Woking) with 1 cap against Wales in 1996.

SENDINGS OFF

Only three players had been sent off playing for Fulham before 1963 in league and cup games. The first player to be sent off for Fulham in the Football League was Willie Walker for retaliation in February 1913 at Bradford Park Avenue. Prior to this George Tutthill had been sent off for retaliation in a Southern League match in 1902 after which he received a 28-day suspension. Johnny McIntyre took an early bath in 1919 and Jack Finch was harshly given his marching orders in 1938.

It has only been since 1985 that players have been sent off on a more regular basis with the likes of Peter Scott and Duncan Jupp having been red-carded on 3 occasions. Scott went against Crystal Palace in September 1985, at Chesterfield in November 1986 and in a play-off match with Bristol Rovers in May 1989. Jupp was sent off against Reading in January 1994, at Colchester in April 1995 and at Rochdale in February 1996.

On 5 occasions two Fulham players have been sent off in the same match. Jeff Hopkins and Gordon Davies as well as coach Jack Burkitt went in a controversial match at Chesterfield in May 1988, while Hopkins again and Kenny Achampong had been sent off at Huddersfield Town in March 1985. Finally Nick Cusack and Martin Thomas received their marching orders in one of many ill-tempered matches at Gillingham in November 1995. Rufus Brevett and Steve Marlet were both sent off at Birmingham in November 2002 and Papa Bouba Diop and Andy Cole were given their marching orders at The Hawthorns in September 2004.

SEQUENCES

Fulham's worst run of defeats is 11 in 1961/62. After beating Blackburn Rovers 2–0 at Ewood Park on 25 November 1961, Fulham did not win another point until 3 March 1962 against Nottingham Forest, 12 matches later.

Fulham's record for the most home wins on the trot is 12. These were the last 8 games of 1958/59 and the first 4 of 1959/60. The worst run of home defeats came in 1961/62 when they lost 7 in succession and the same season saw Fulham's worst run without scoring a goal at home when they failed to score in 4 consecutive games at Craven Cottage.

The longest spell the Whites have gone without scoring a goal came early in 1968/69. After Jim Conway's 3rd minute goal at Villa Park on 17 August, Fulham did not score again for 660 minutes until Malcolm Macdonald's 32nd minute winner against Crystal Palace on Friday 13 September; after 6 goalless matches.

CONSECUTIVE MATCHES

Les Barrett holds the Fulham record for consecutive Football League appearances with 149 between 1969 and 1972. The run started in a 2–1 victory over Gillingham on 23 August 1969 and ended on 11 November 1972 at Hull City. Close behind is Maik Taylor who made 146 consecutive appearances in goal for Fulham between March 1998 and April 2011 when Marcus Hahnemann took his place and Taylor moved to the bench for one game.

Maik is followed in third place by Ernie Beecham with 122 between 1926 and 1928 – Ernie made his league debut in goal at Blackpool in December 1925 and did not miss a game until receiving a terrible injury diving at the feet of an Exeter forward called Death in November 1928. Sadly, Ernie was never the same after this mishap.

Another goalkeeper, Arthur Reynolds, is fourth with 120 consecutive matches between May 1920 and March 1924. This is a long way behind the Football League record set by Harold Bell between August 1946 and August 1955 when he played 401 consecutive League matches for Tranmere Rovers.

The record for consecutive appearances in league and cup competitions for Fulham is 167 by Les Barrett, John Dempsey (136), Barry Lloyd (135), Ernie Beecham (130) Arthur Reynolds (129) and Billy Goldie (128). Taylor does not come into this category as he missed some Worthington Cup matches at the beginning of 2000/01 season.

SHORTEST CAREERS

Eight players share the distinction of having the shortest
Fulham careers, making only one substitute appearance in the
League, FA Cup or League Cup. The first of these was Hugh
Cunningham who replaced George Cohen for the second
half against Leicester City in January 1968. Danny O'Leary
replaced Johnny Haynes at Bristol Rovers in September 1969
and Gary Smith played for 20 minutes in a Fulham shirt at
Oldham Athletic in May 1986. Steve Greaves made a brief
appearance at Chesterfield in May 1988 and John Gregory
replaced Lee Harrison in goal when he was sent off against
Hartlepool in April 1995 after 30 minutes. Andy Arnott was
a playing substitute against Bournemouth in February 1998
but also played a couple of games in the Auto Windscreens
Shield. Finally and most recently François Keller played for
18 minutes in a Fulham shirt as substitute against Burnley
at the Cottage in December 1998 with one other appearance
coming in the Football League Trophy. Keller returned to
Strasbourg in the close season of 1999.

MOST APPEARANCES

Fulham's most loyal player, Johnny Haynes, heads the list of
league appearance makers with 594 for the Whites between
1952 and 1970. Eddie Lowe is some way behind with 473
from 1950 to 1963, followed by Frank Penn (427), Les
Barrett (420+3), John Marshall (395+18), George Cohen 408
and Len Oliver 406. The maestro Haynes also appeared in 44

FA Cup ties and 20 League Cup matches giving him a grand total of 658 appearances for Fulham.

TRANSFERS (INCOMING)

Fulham's first transfer over £1,000 came in November 1907 when Fred Harrison and Fred Mouncher were signed from Southampton for a joint fee. Barney Travers broke this record in February 1921 when he was signed from Sunderland for £3,000 while Jack McDonald was the first £10,000+ player in June 1948 when he was transferred from Bournemouth for £12,000. Three-and-a-half years later Bobby Brennan arrived for £20,000 from Birmingham City. Allan Clarke was Fulham's first signing over £30,000, coming from Walsall in March 1966, and the unfortunate Frank Large (valued at £50,000) was part of a deal which took Clarke to Leicester City in June 1968.

Teddy Maybank and Peter Kitchen held the incoming record transfer fee of £150,000 for 18 years before Fulham signed Paul Moody for £200,000 in July 1997. The record has been broken a number of times since – Paul Peschisolido signed for £1.1m from West Bromwich Albion in October 1997 but this was quickly broken with the arrival of Chris Coleman for £2.1m the following month. The record was beaten again when Lee Clark cost £3m when he joined Fulham from Sunderland in July 1999 and the £4m signing of Alain Goma from Newcastle United to Fulham in March 2001 was soon beaten twice in quick succession when first Edwin van der Sar arrived from Juventus for £7m and a week or two later Steven Marlet was transferred from Lyon for £11.5m in August 2001. This remains the record in 2012.

TRANSFERS (OUTGOING)

Fulham have often had to sell players in the past to alleviate their poor financial position. The first of these was England international Frank Osborne who was sold to Spurs for a record fee of £3,000 in January 1924 but this record was broken in August 1928 when Sid Elliott was sold to neighbours Chelsea for £3,600. This record held until July 1950 when Fulham sold Arthur Rowley to Leicester City for £12,000. Bobby Robson broke this record again when he moved to West Bromwich Albion For £25,000 in March 1956 and Alan Mullery did it again when he was transferred to Spurs in March 1964 for a massive £72,000. Allan Clarke set a new record when he moved to Leicester City for £150,000 in June 1968 but the record went again when Paul Went was sold to Pompey for £155,000 in December 1973 to ease a financial crisis at the club.

Teddy Maybank moved to Brighton for £237,000 in November 1977 and Richard Money was to hold the record for an outgoing transfer from Fulham for 18 years after his move to Liverpool in April 1980 for £333,333. The record was finally beaten by Tony Thorpe when Fulham sold him to Bristol City for £1m in June 1998. This record was smashed in January 2004 when Louis Saha was sold to Manchester United for £12.8m.

WELSH INTERNATIONALS

Fulham now have 12 players who have represented Wales while appearing for Fulham. The numbers have swelled in recent years by the inclusion of Kit Symons, Chris Coleman. Andy Melville, Paul Trollope, Mark Pembridge, Mark Crossley and Simon Davies. Gordon Davies played for Wales 15 times and is closely followed by Jeff Hopkins who played for his country 14 times. Also capped while at the Cottage are Cliff Jones, Billy Richards and Sid Thomas. Taffy O'Callaghan, Peter O'Sullivan, Eddie Perry, Dicky Richards, Alan Neilson and Dave Roberts all played for Wales before or after leaving the club.

EUROPA LEAGUE DREAM

Fulham surprised the football world by reaching the final of the Europa League in 2010 after a run of 18 matches which started back in late July. It all ended in tears with Diego Forlan's 117th-minute winner in Hamburg ending Fulham's dreams of glory. Forlan was the Spanish team's hero, scoring both of Atlético Madrid's goals with Simon Davies hitting an equaliser for the Whites to bring on extra time.

There were many highlights on the way. After qualifying round victories over FK Vėtra and Amkar Perm to reach the group stage, Fulham needed to beat Basle in the final group game in Switzerland to reach the knockout stage. The match was played in freezing conditions but Bobby Zamora put Fulham 2–0 up after converting two crosses from Bjørn Helge

Riise. Alex Frei pulled a goal back for the Swiss but Zoltán Gera added Fulham's third and despite a late goal from Basle, the Whites held on for victory.

Fulham were often outplayed by Shakhtar Donetsk in the first round of their knockout stage encounter, but Bobby Zamora's great 25-yard shot saw Fulham to a 2–1 victory. Fulham were up against it in the next round after that had lost 3–1 to Italian giants Juventus in Turin. Things looked grim when Trezeguet gave Juve the lead in the return leg after two minutes but in one of the greatest games at the Cottage, Fulham remarkably went on to win 4–1 and clinched the tie 5–4 on aggregate. Clint Dempsey scored a superb goal to win the tie when he hit home a stunning lofted chip.

In the next round Fulham saw off Wolfsburg, winning home and away to reach the semi-final where they met SV Hamburg. After a 0–0 draw in Germany, Hamburg took the lead at the Cottage when Petrić scored in the first half. Simon Davies equalised before Zoltán Gera hit the winner 14 minutes from time. Although Fulham ultimately lost in the final it was a great moment in the club's history to reach a European final.

FULHAM'S RISE TO THE PREMIER LEAGUE

In January 1996, Fulham lost at Torquay United to hit the 91st spot in the Football League and look non-league football in the face. However, in a remarkable period in the club's history, by August 2001 they were playing their football in the Premier League. The following season,

1996/97, new manager Micky Adams transformed the club with only modest spending as they finished runners-up to Wigan Athletic – a vital 2–1 victory at Carlisle in early April followed by a 0–0 draw at Mansfield three days later meant that Fulham had clinched promotion. They would have won the title that season but lost their next game 1–0 at home to Northampton Town.

Soon afterwards, Mohamed Al Fayed took over as owner and chairman of the club and promised rapid promotion with the aim of Premier League football. Kevin Keegan took over as manager in 1998 and the following season Fulham walked away with the Second Division championship. They won 31 of their 46 games and clinched a record 101 points in the process. Keegan left to become the England manager and after a unsuccessful period under the management of Paul Bracewell, Fayed appointed Jean Tigana to the hot seat in 2000. It was an inspired move and he soon signed future stars Louis Saha and Louis Boa Morte. Saha hit 27 goals in 2000/01, with Boa Morte and Barry Hayles also hitting 18 goals as Fulham walked away with the First Division title. They had won the first 11 games of the season and again ended the season on 101 points.

The club were allowed to play at Craven Cottage for the next season as they consolidated their Premiership status. Tigana brought in more star names when he signed Dutch International goalkeeper Edwin van der Sar from Juventus and Steed Malbranque, Steve Marlet and Alain Goma from French football.

Also available from The History Press

The Men Who Made Fulham Football Club
Alex White
978-0-7524-2423-1

Images of Sport: Fulham FC
Alex White
978-0-7524-4450-5

**Visit our website and discover thousands of other
History Press books.**

www.thehistorypress.co.uk